INTRODUCING
ISSUES WITH
OPPOSING
VIEWPOINTS®

Cyberbullying

Lauri Scherer, *Book Editor*

GREENHAVEN PRESS
A part of Gale, Cengage Learning

GALE
CENGAGE Learning·

Farmington Hills, Mich • San Francisco • New York • Waterville, Maine
Meriden, Conn • Mason, Ohio • Chicago

Patricia Coryell, *Vice President & Publisher, New Products & GVRL*
Douglas Dentino, *Manager, New Products*
Judy Galens, *Acquisitions Editor*

For more information, contact:
Greenhaven Press
27500 Drake Rd.
Farmington Hills, MI 48331-3535
Or you can visit our Internet site at gale.cengage.com

For product information and technology assistance, contact us at

Gale Customer Support, 1-800-877-4253
For permission to use material from this text or product, submit all requests online at www.cengage.com/permissions

Further permissions questions can be e-mailed to permissionrequest@cengage.com

Articles in Greenhaven Press anthologies are often edited for length to meet page requirements. In addition, original titles of these works are changed to clearly present the main thesis and to explicitly indicate the author's opinion. Every effort is made to ensure that Greenhaven Press accurately reflects the original intent of the authors. Every effort has been made to trace the owners of copyrighted material.

Cover image © SpeedKingz/Shutterstock.com.

LIBRARY OF CONGRESS CATALOGING-IN-PUBLICATION DATA

Cyberbullying / Lauri S. Scherer, book editor.
    pages cm. -- (Introducing issues with opposing viewpoints)
  Includes bibliographical references and index.
  ISBN 978-0-7377-7234-0 (hardcover)
  1. Cyberbullying--Juvenile literature. 2. Internet and teenagers--Juvenile literature.
  3. Bullying--Juvenile literature. I. Scherer, Lauri S.
    HV6773.15.C92C935 2015
    302.34'302854678--dc23

                                        2014030230

Printed in the United States of America
2 3 4 5 6 7 19 18 17 16 15

Contents

Chapter 3: How Can Cyberbullying Be Prevented?

Foreword

Indulging in a wide spectrum of ideas, beliefs, and perspectives is a critical cornerstone of democracy. After all, it is often debates over differences of opinion, such as whether to legalize abortion, how to treat prisoners, or when to enact the death penalty, that shape our society and drive it forward. Such diversity of thought is frequently regarded as the hallmark of a healthy and civilized culture. As the Reverend Clifford Schutjer of the First Congregational Church in Mansfield, Ohio, declared in a 2001 sermon, "Surrounding oneself with only like-minded people, restricting what we listen to or read only to what we find agreeable is irresponsible. Refusing to entertain doubts once we make up our minds is a subtle but deadly form of arrogance." With this advice in mind, Introducing Issues with Opposing Viewpoints books aim to open readers' minds to the critically divergent views that comprise our world's most important debates.

Introducing Issues with Opposing Viewpoints simplifies for students the enormous and often overwhelming mass of material now available via print and electronic media. Collected in every volume is an array of opinions that captures the essence of a particular controversy or topic. Introducing Issues with Opposing Viewpoints books embody the spirit of nineteenth-century journalist Charles A. Dana's axiom: "Fight for your opinions, but do not believe that they contain the whole truth, or the only truth." Absorbing such contrasting opinions teaches students to analyze the strength of an argument and compare it to its opposition. From this process readers can inform and strengthen their own opinions, or be exposed to new information that will change their minds. Introducing Issues with Opposing Viewpoints is a mosaic of different voices. The authors are statesmen, pundits, academics, journalists, corporations, and ordinary people who have felt compelled to share their experiences and ideas in a public forum. Their words have been collected from newspapers, journals, books, speeches, interviews, and the Internet, the fastest growing body of opinionated material in the world.

Introducing Issues with Opposing Viewpoints shares many of the well-known features of its critically acclaimed parent series, Opposing Viewpoints. The articles are presented in a pro/con format, allowing readers to absorb divergent perspectives side by side. Active reading questions preface each viewpoint, requiring the student to approach the material thoughtfully and carefully. Useful charts, graphs, and cartoons supplement each article. A thorough introduction provides readers with crucial background on an issue. An annotated bibliography points the reader toward articles, books, and websites that contain additional information on the topic. An appendix of organizations to contact contains a wide variety of charities, nonprofit organizations, political groups, and private enterprises that each hold a position on the issue at hand. Finally, a comprehensive index allows readers to locate content quickly and efficiently.

Introducing Issues with Opposing Viewpoints is also significantly different from Opposing Viewpoints. As the series title implies, its presentation will help introduce students to the concept of opposing viewpoints and learn to use this material to aid in critical writing and debate. The series' four-color, accessible format makes the books attractive and inviting to readers of all levels. In addition, each viewpoint has been carefully edited to maximize a reader's understanding of the content. Short but thorough viewpoints capture the essence of an argument. A substantial, thought-provoking essay question placed at the end of each viewpoint asks the student to further investigate the issues raised in the viewpoint, compare and contrast two authors' arguments, or consider how one might go about forming an opinion on the topic at hand. Each viewpoint contains sidebars that include at-a-glance information and handy statistics. A Facts About section located in the back of the book further supplies students with relevant facts and figures.

Following in the tradition of the Opposing Viewpoints series, Greenhaven Press continues to provide readers with invaluable exposure to the controversial issues that shape our world. As John Stuart Mill once wrote: "The only way in which a human being can make some approach to knowing the whole of a subject is by hearing what can be said about it by persons of every variety of opinion and studying all modes in which it can be looked at by every character of mind. No wise man ever acquired his wisdom in any mode but this." It is to this principle that Introducing Issues with Opposing Viewpoints books are dedicated.

Introduction

"We should demand more from these sites, by holding them accountable for enforcing their own rules."

—Emily Bazelon, "How to Stop the Bullies," *The Atlantic,* March 2013

When people talk about how to address the problem of cyberbullying, they usually focus on two main solutions: making parents responsible for monitoring their children's Internet use or making schools responsible for monitoring their students' interactions and taking appropriate disciplinary action. But increasingly, certain voices are calling for another party to bear responsibility: the social media and other websites where such bullying plays out.

All social media websites have at least some prohibitions on bullying, harassment, defamation, and other forms of hateful or criminal speech, yet the extent to which these are defined and enforced varies. Some sites claim it is impossible to monitor every post or uploaded content for bullying messages, because it is not always clear whether a message is actually negative unless one knows the context. "Bullying is hard," says Dave Willner, who works for Facebook's Hate and Harassment Team, which determines the validity of millions of user complaint reports. "It's slippery to define, and it's even harder when it's writing instead of speech. Tone of voice disappears."[1]

Teams like Willner's have a very difficult task when trying to determine what qualifies as cyberbullying; with 2.5 billion new pieces of content uploaded to such sites each day, it is easy for material to resist detection. Yet some argue that social media websites have both the obligation and ability to improve on their process. "Are we really expected to believe that the outsize creative minds that made this technology possible are such failures when it comes to integrating it into human lives in a humane fashion?" argues Jane McKenna, a Canadian politician who has made the fight against cyberbullying a feature of her political service. "Just as the scientists who gave us the atomic bomb felt compelled to dedicate the second act of their lives to peace, the programming community that has engineered these tools should bear some measure of responsibility for the world it creates."[2]

One way social media websites have sought to cut down on harmful content is to make users more identifiable. The hope is to prevent anonymous account creation and posting, which is a main source of the problem. Indeed people of all ages tend to be meaner when they have the opportunity to communicate anonymously: A 2014 study by researchers at the University of Houston of comments on the Internet found that more than half (53 percent) of all anonymous comments featured language that was racist, profane, vulgar, or hateful, while only 29 percent of comments in which the author was identified were offensive. Although Facebook requires users to identify themselves (though many users easily get around such requirements) others, such as Secret, Whisper, and Yik Yak explicitly require that users be anonymous, and some exist solely for the point of harassing and bullying other people. Requiring sites to collect and display users' real information and making it more difficult for users to circumvent these requirements could thus be one way to cut down on content that feeds cyberbullying.

Another way social media sites could cut down on cyberbullying, some critics say, is to improve the way in which they identify problematic posting. To do this, they need to develop very sophisticated algorithms, complex computer formulas that are the lifeblood of such technology. Such an attempt is under way at the Massachusetts Institute of Technology (MIT), where researchers are working to build an algorithm that could flag problematic content before it is ever posted. Under the direction of computer scientist Henry Lieberman, researchers analyzed thousands of YouTube comments and videos and over a million Formspring posts that were flagged for bullying. Lieberman's team identified six themes that ran through nearly all the offensive posts: race, intelligence, appearance, ethnicity, sexuality, and social acceptance/rejection. Lieberman asserts that "95 percent of the posts were about those six topics."[3]

Lieberman's team then built a database called BullySpace that not only recognizes words that would obviously be used in a bullying context (such as "ugly" or "slut") but also more-nuanced conversation that could potentially be hurtful to a specific person or in a particular context. BullySpace caught about 80 percent of the insulting or bullying posts that were caught by human monitors. Lieberman and other computer scientists are working toward perfecting an algorithm that is sufficiently sophisticated and nuanced to catch the types of cyberbullying content that are likely to turn into "pile-ups," where one post, comment, or video collects hateful comments at an alarming speed; these are among the most destructive cyberbullying incidents.

Whether such methods can successfully cut down on cyberbullying is one issue; whether companies will move to employ them is another. Doing so could be expensive to develop and deploy and could also cost sites subscribers and thus advertising. McKenna and others argue that sites have an obligation to do so despite the expense, however, because of the way in which Internet technology enables horrible and unlawful activity. "If new technology makes it easier to be a stalker, rapist or abusive ex-partner; if it made it possible to slander or smear the innocent; if it gave immature youths the power to issue threats, the leverage to drive children into spirals of depression that ended in institutions, hospitals or morgues," contends McKenna, "is that not something of concern, even from a bottom-line profit standpoint?"[4]

The role social media companies should play in preventing cyberbullying is just one of the many perspectives considered in *Introducing Issues with Opposing Viewpoints: Cyberbullying.* Well-argued pairs debate how serious the problem of cyberbullying is, how society should respond to it, and how it can be prevented. Noted experts and media commentators offer compelling perspectives on the subject, while reading comprehension questions and thought-provoking essay prompts encourage students to form their own opinions on the matter. Sources for further reading on the topic and organizations to contact round out this volume on this timely topic.

Notes

1. Quoted in Emily Bazelon, "How to Stop the Bullies," *The Atlantic,* March 2013. www.theatlantic.com.
2. Jane McKenna, "Can Technology Batter Bullying? Social Media Worsened It, Now Let Them Help Stop It," *The Spectator,* November 7, 2011. www.spectator.co.uk.
3. Quoted in Bazelon, "How to Stop the Bullies."
4. McKenna, "Can Technology Batter Bullying?"

Chapter 1

Is Cyberbullying a Serious Problem?

While statistics vary on how widespread cyberbullying is, most experts agree that it is a real issue among young people today.

Viewpoint

1

Cyberbullying Is Epidemic

John Stephens

In the following viewpoint, John Stephens argues that cyberbullying has become a deadly epidemic in the United States. He maintains that the effects of cyberbullying are more severe than traditional bullying because it is harder for the victim to escape. Social media play an important role in the lives of young people, the author contends, but they enable cyberbullies to torment their victims 24/7. Stephens believes fighting cyberbullying requires a coordinated effort among schools, parents, and communities to teach kids about the risks of social media and the dangers of cyberbullying. Stephens is a senior vice president for Keenan and Associates, insurance consultants who work with more than six hundred California public school districts to provide resources and programs to keep children safe online and educate them about the risks of cyberbullying.

> *"Cyberbullying has become an epidemic in this country."*

AS YOU READ, CONSIDER THE FOLLOWING QUESTIONS:

1. According to the author, youth aged eight to eighteen spend how many hours a day "plugged in"?
2. What percentage of middle-school students reported that they have contemplated attempting suicide, according to Stephens?

What do Ryan, Megan, Seth, Phoebe and Tyler have in common? These are teenagers who committed suicide due to cyberbullying. These deaths have put the spotlight on the growing problem of cyberbullying and sparked more calls for tougher action. This issue has received so much attention that President Barack Obama held a White House conference on bullying [in March 2011] and subsequently launched StopBullying.gov, a website to help prevent and stop bullying.

Cyberbullying has become an epidemic in this country. The new generation of kids are growing up on the web and defining their own cultural rules. A recent study by the Kaiser Family Foundation reported that kids ages 8 to 18 now spend an average of seven and a half hours a day "plugged-in"—online, on the phone, or in the thrall of TV or some other electronic device. And in a random survey conducted by the Cyberbullying Research Center, 20% of middle-school students reported that they seriously contemplated attempting suicide. There is an upward suicide trend in the 10 to 19 year-old age group and the correlating factor is bullying and cyberbullying. The death rate is climbing and many are questioning whether or not the digital age has made the younger generation callous.

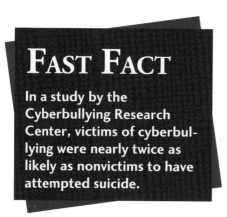

FAST FACT

In a study by the Cyberbullying Research Center, victims of cyberbullying were nearly twice as likely as nonvictims to have attempted suicide.

Cyberbullying Is a Silent Epidemic

The effects of cyberbullying can be more severe than those of "traditional" bullying because a child who is targeted may see no escape and no place to hide. When bullying hits the internet, it morphs out of control. There are far more witnesses to cyberbullying and the reality now is that cyberbullies never sleep.

United States Department Education Secretary Arne Duncan is calling bullying a "silent epidemic" and [saying] that bullying involving race, religion or sexual orientation may be a federal offense. This issue has become global and as cyberbullying gains more media attention, lawsuits are increasing. Headlines such as "Families seeking $35 million in bullying lawsuits" and "Court awards bullied student $800,000" have become common weekly news. Another widely publicized lawsuit was a boy who sued the fathers of three former

Most Adults Consider Physical Bullying and Cyberbullying Equally Dangerous

Which is more dangerous: physical bullying or cyberbullying?

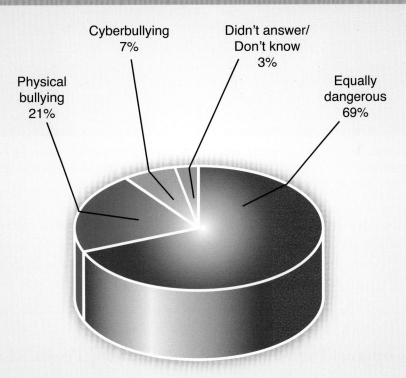

Cyberbullying
7%

Didn't answer/
Don't know
3%

Physical
bullying
21%

Equally
dangerous
69%

Note: Data from "Most Adults Say Physical Bullying, Cyber Bullying Are Equally Dangerous," Rasmussen Reports, October 2010.

Taken from: Thomas J. Billitteri, "Preventing Bullying," *CQ Researcher*, vol. 20, no. 43, December 10, 2010.

A teen and young boy watch a laptop monitor in their living room. The Internet plays an important part in young people's lives, with some kids spending many hours a day plugged in to social media and other online sites.

classmates for $350,000 after they obtained a copy of a video the boy made for a class project and posted it on the internet. The video depicted the boy using a golf club as a light saber; he was dubbed the "Starwars Kid" and received world-wide ridicule. The suit settled out of court.

The Internet Plays a Powerful Role in Young People's Lives

The Internet is incredibly powerful and has transformed this generation. However, it's hard to imagine that such a vast resource could be used for such terrible deeds. Social media has an enormous effect on the lives of young people who often share pieces of their life with their social networking friends that they normally would not bring up during face to face conversations. Internet safety expert and privacy lawyer Parry Aftab said types of bullying amounts to torture for some kids. "The schoolyard bullies beat you up and then go home," she said. "The cyberbullies beat you up at home, at grandma's house or wherever you're connected to technology."

Personally, I don't believe kids post derogatory comments with catastrophic intent. However, it's becoming more and more evident that some kids do not understand the consequences of their actions. The prosecution of the nine kids in Phoebe Prince's suicide, or Tyler Clementi's of Rutgers University death, clearly reminds us of the growing dangers of social media.

Ending This Tragic Epidemic

Social media risks such as cyberbullying and sexting are growing problems facing children, families and schools. As these risks become more prevalent, many are wondering how to police these behaviors. Should a school get involved when young kids bully each other online? They certainly would if the bullying occurred at school and in some cases the school will become involved with bullying outside of school as well. Schools are in a precarious position because we now see many examples in the media where schools have been sued because they took action against a student when they shouldn't have or they failed to take action when they were supposed to.

In the 21st century, the Internet plays an important part of kids' lives, though the boundaries between real life and virtual life are blurry. It's important to teach kids proactively about the serious risks of social media and the long term consequences of their online behaviors. This requires a coordinated effort of schools, parents and communities to talk about the inherent dangers of cyberbullying, sexting and other social media risks.

We are in the infancy stages of the social media dangers epidemic. Gone are the days when the schoolyard bullies beat you up and went home. Gone are the days when kids teased one another and it ended with giggles and at worst, a few tears. We are living in a world where bullies can reach you anywhere and anytime and where humiliation is shared at the click a mouse to a widespread audience. The 21st century affords incredible opportunities, but it's also brought us social media dangers and far too many young tragedies. It's time to stop this epidemic.

EVALUATING THE AUTHOR'S ARGUMENTS

In this viewpoint, John Stephens argues that cyberbullying is a deadly epidemic and that the effects of cyberbullying are more harmful than traditional bullying. Do you agree with his assertion that cyberbullying is more severe than traditional bullying? Why or why not?

Cyberbullying Is Not Epidemic

Larry Magid

"Rather than an epidemic, bullying is actually on the decline."

In the following viewpoint, Larry Magid maintains that cyberbullying is not epidemic and that there is no cause for public panic. In contrast to the public narrative, Magid argues that bullying is actually on the decline. Most teens say they have not been cyberbullied, he contends. While cyberbullying is an issue in society, the author believes that labeling it as epidemic is inaccurate and only worsens the problem. Magid is an Internet safety advocate, codirector of ConnectSafely.org, founder of SafeKids.com and SafeTeens.com, and a board member of the National Center for Missing and Exploited Children.

AS YOU READ, CONSIDER THE FOLLOWING QUESTIONS:
1. According to the author, what percentage of teens has experienced some type of bullying or harassment from their peers?
2. Magid states that what percentage of teens would not forward an embarrassing e-mail about someone else?
3. What is the best strategy to fight cyberbullying, according to the author?

Recent [April 2010] stories in the press about teenage cyber-bullying and real-world bullying are sickening. It's hard to know how much cyberbullying contributed to her decision to kill herself, but the case of Phoebe Prince brings tears to my eyes. The South Hadley, Mass., 15-year-old was reportedly the brunt of repeated cruelty at the hands of classmates (six of whom are now facing criminal charges) until she put an end to her life.

There is also the recent cyberbullying case of Alexis Pilkington, a 17-year-old girl from Long Island, N.Y., who committed suicide last month [March 2010] after being taunted with cruel comments on the Web site FormSpring.me. Some of those comments reportedly even continued after her death.

And there are countless more bullying and cyberbullying cases that don't make headlines. But even though the overwhelming majority of children are able to "survive" being bullied doesn't mean that it's not painful. I still have emotional scars from being bullied when I was a teen.

Cases like these have contributed to what's starting to look like a bullying panic, not unlike the predator panic of a few years ago that caused people to worry (in most cases needlessly) about their children being sexually molested by someone they meet online. Those were great headlines and sound bites for politicians, but the research showed that it just wasn't the case for the vast majority of youth. While it is true that kids are many times more likely to be bullied and cyberbullied than sexually molested by online strangers, we need to put this issue into some perspective. Yes, we should be concerned, but there is no cause for panic.

FAST FACT

According to the *Huffington Post*, it is believed that the term *cyberbullying* was coined by Canadian Bill Belsey from the words *cyberspace* and *bullying*.

Bullying Is on the Decline

As prominent as it is, bullying and cyberbullying are not the norm. Most young people want no part of bullying and consider it reprehensible behavior. Depending on what study you read, anywhere from

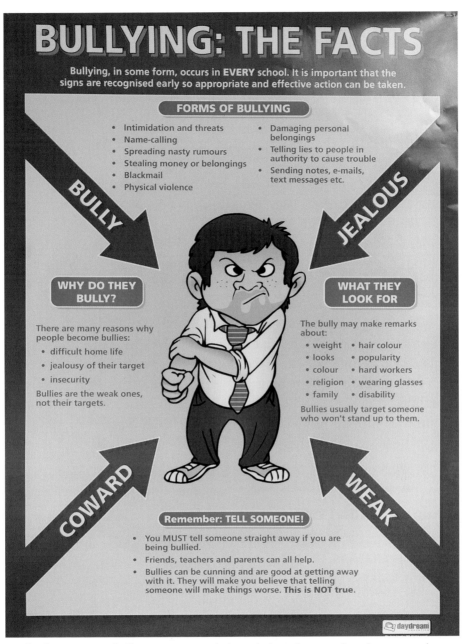

A school poster paints bullies in a negative light and also informs students how to stand up against bullying when they see it or hear about it.

15 percent to 30 percent of teens say they have experienced some type of bullying or harassment from their peers.

And when it comes to bullying in general, the trend is moving in the right direction. Rather than an epidemic, bullying is actually on the decline. A study published last month in the *Archives of Pediatric and Adolescent Medicine* found that the percentage of youth ([ages] 2 to 17 years old) reporting physical bullying in the past year went down from 22 percent in 2003 to 15 percent in 2008.

A national study of youth commissioned by the Girl Scouts came to a similar conclusion. Young people are actually more responsible, more involved in their community, and more tolerant of diversity than they were 20 years ago. The survey found that 84 percent of youth said they wouldn't forward an embarrassing e-mail about someone else; 6 percent said they would. That's 6 percent too many but still a relatively small minority.

Not all surveys have the same results. In February, the Cyberbullying Research Center polled 4,000 teenagers from a large U.S. school district and found that 15.9 percent of boys and 25.8 percent of girls reported having been cyberbullied at some point in their life. Among the boys, 7.1 percent said they had been cyberbullied in the last 30 days and 7.9 percent of girls had been victims during that time period. When combining genders, overall 20.7 percent of teens say they've been cyberbullied in their lifetimes with 7.4 percent saying they were cyberbullied in the past 30 days. A survey conducted last year by Cox Communications found that approximately 19 percent of teens say they've been cyberbullied online or via text message and that 10 percent say they've cyberbullied someone else.

Looking at the Positive Side

There is no question that there is a problem and I certainly don't want sugarcoat it, but it's also important to look at it from the positive side as well. It's worth pointing out that about 80 percent of teens say they have not been cyberbullied while 90 percent of teens say they haven't cyberbullied other teens.

Posing the issue in the positive is not just a silly math trick—it's actually a strategy that can help reduce bullying or, at least marginalize those who engage in it.

In a paper . . . presented at the 2008 National Conference on the Social Norms Approach, H. Wesley Perkins and David Craig reported on a survey of more than 52,000 students from 78 secondary schools and concluded that "while bullying is substantial, it is not the norm."

"I'd love to, dude, but I've got, like, another solid hour of bullying to do."

They went on to say that "the most common (and erroneous) perception, however, is that the majority engage in and support such behavior." The reason that this is an important observation is because, as the researchers found, the "perceptions of bullying behaviors are highly predictive of personal bullying behavior." Even though the "norm is not to bully," only a minority of young people realize that. If kids think that bullying is common or "normal," they are more likely to be bullies.

Based on this research, the commonly held belief that we are going through an "epidemic" of bullying or cyberbullying is not only inaccurate, but it is likely contributing to the problem.

A better strategy is to try to convince young people that bullying is not only wrong and unacceptable but is abnormal behavior, practiced by a small group of outliers. Taking it a step further, how can we marginalize bullies so that they—not their victims—are seen as losers and how can we enlist young people themselves to stand up against bullying when they see it or hear about it.

Adults Are Role Models

Adults need to be good role models. Politicians need to think about this the next time they consider demonizing (as opposed to criticizing) an opponent. Media personalities and talk show hosts need to think about the messages they're giving to children when they engage in name calling. We all need to be aware of comments we make in the presence of children and even people who comment on blogs need to think about the difference between legitimate criticism and derision. Children learn by observing our behavior, and there are plenty of adults who behave like bullies.

Changing behavior isn't easy, but it's not impossible. I've been watching episodes of the TV show Mad Men, which is set in the 1960s when it was acceptable to smoke around other people, ride in cars without seat belts, leave trash everywhere, make derogatory comments about minorities, and treat women as inferior beings. We haven't yet completely eliminated any of those dangerous or antisocial behaviors, but we've come a long way. With concerted effort and national leadership, we can do the same with bullying.

EVALUATING THE AUTHOR'S ARGUMENTS

In this viewpoint, Larry Magid claims that cyberbullying is not epidemic and panic is unwarranted. Whose argument is more convincing, Magid's or John Stephens's, the author of the previous viewpoint? Explain your answer.

Cyberbullying Is More Common than Traditional Bullying

Raychelle Cassada Lohmann

"Cyber-bullying is done impul-sively and not planned out like tra-ditional bullying."

In the following viewpoint, Raychelle Cassada Lohmann maintains that cyber-bullying occurs more often than traditional bullying does. The author defines cyberbul-lying and compares its characteristics to traditional bullying. Cyberbullying greatly affects youth, she contends, and can have a severe impact on the victim's life. The author believes the key to fighting cyberbul-lying is teaching youth how to use technol-ogy appropriately and warning them about online dangers. Lohmann is a counselor in North and South Carolina and the author of *The Anger Workbook for Teens* and *The Bullying Workbook for Teens*.

AS YOU READ, CONSIDER THE FOLLOWING QUESTIONS:

1. According to a study cited by the author, what percentage of youth has admitted to experiencing or taking part in cyberbullying?
2. What characteristics of traditional bullying are not applicable in cyberbullying, as stated by the author?

J ust how different is traditional bullying from cyberbullying? Studies are beginning to show that the way youth bully online is a lot different from traditional schoolyard bullying. Teens may think what they are posting or texting is just a joke, but if you're on the receiving end it may not be all that funny. In fact, if the "joking" is repetitive, it could cross the line into bullying, more specifically cyberbullying. According to the American Academy of Pediatrics cyberbullying is the "most common online risk for all teens and is a peer to peer risk."

According to a [2012] study released by the University of British Columbia cyberbullying is a big problem, even more common than traditional bullying. About 25 to 30 percent of the young people surveyed admitted experiencing or taking part in cyberbullying, but only 12 percent said the same about traditional bullying. To top it off, 95 percent of the youth said that what happened online was meant to be a joke and about 5 percent was actually meant to harm someone. So, what makes cyberbullying so different from traditional bullying?

Comparing Bullying and Cyberbullying

In traditional bullying you're usually working with a bully, victim or bystander but that's not the case in cyberbullying. In fact, it's not uncommon to play multiple roles such as cyberbully, target and witness. Previous research indicates that cyberbullying is rarely premeditated like traditional bullying, where the bully plans his or her line of attack. In many cases cyberbullying is done impulsively and not planned out like in traditional bullying where the bully pre-meditates the next attack. Also, traditional bullying has the following characteristics that may not be present in cyberbullying cases:

• a need for power and control
• proactively targeting the victim
• aggression

A father and daughter look at content on a digital tablet together. Parents and other adults should teach young people about responsible online behavior and how joking or insensitive comments may harm recipients.

So, just what is cyberbullying? By definition, it's the deliberate and repeated harm inflicted through the use of cell phones/smartphones, computers/tablets, and other electronic devices (including Wi-Fi gaming devices). It's an easier way to bully because unlike traditional bullying it doesn't involve face to face interaction. Teens can become desensitized to a computer screen, and say or do things they wouldn't do to a person's face. The computer desensitizes teens and decreases the level of empathy they feel toward the victim. Plus, when they can't see the person's reaction to what they post or text they may not know if they've gone too far.

Cyberbullying Hurts

It appears that today's youth don't equate joking around with bullying. Even though they do it jokingly it can cut the receiver deeply. By definition a joke is something that is supposed to, but here's the magic question, "who's laughing?" Ask any teen who's been cyberbullied and they probably won't see the humor in the situation. Plus, when something is posted online, it can be humiliating. That old saying "www" means the "whole world's watching" holds true and cyberbullying victims know it. Bottom line is cyberbullying hurts.

Just imagine. . .

You get a text from a friend to check out someone's page, you go there and see degrading posts and a crude picture of you in a swimsuit that had been Photoshopped. Following the posts are a string of lewd comments. You start getting text after text from people, some you don't even know, saying mean things about the post. It feels like the world is laughing at you only you're not laughing. You dread going to school the next day because you have to face all of these people. Your stomach is churning and your head is pounding. You pray it will just go away, like it never happened. "MAKE IT STOP, Make It Stop, make it stop," screams through your mind. You have just entered into the world of a victim. What may have started as a mean joke crossed the line into something more severe, cyberbullying. Scenarios like this are just one example of how some teens are misusing technology.

Young people can quickly spread a rumor through texting, taping an embarrassing incident and posting it on YouTube, or uploading pictures or unkind comments on social networking sites. There are many different avenues that can be used to cyberbully. The key to decreasing cyberbullying is educating today's youth to think before they click. One wrong click has the power to change someone's life forever.

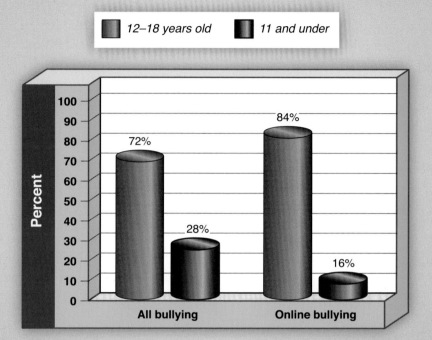

Cyberbullying Affects an Older Age Group

■ 12–18 years old   ■ 11 and under

Percent

	All bullying	Online bullying

- 72% (All bullying, 12–18 years old)
- 28% (All bullying, 11 and under)
- 84% (Online bullying, 12–18 years old)
- 16% (Online bullying, 11 and under)

Taken from: Ami Sedghi, "Cyberbullying Contacts to Childline up by 87%," *The Guardian*, January 9, 2014.

Protecting Teens from Online Dangers

Teaching teens to protect themselves online is very important. I compare learning how to drive a car to teaching teens how to use technology. Here's my logic, odds are you wouldn't turn your teen loose with the keys to the car if they haven't been properly trained or educated to operate a vehicle. Why? Because it's dangerous! He could kill himself or someone else. Well, we should realize that the wonderful cyber world also possesses dangers. The internet highway can be dangerous if teens post inappropriate material, bully, give out personal information to strangers, etc. So we really need to educate our teens about how to use technology appropriately. Just as you probably wouldn't toss the car keys at an inexperienced teen and tell him to go take a spin, you shouldn't place a smartphone or any other electronic device with internet capability in his hands without making sure that he knows how to use it properly.

Let's help our teens realize that feelings do exist in the cyber world, manners do matter, and most importantly, there's a real life person on the receiving end of the messages. . . . A person who laughs, cries and hurts, just like we do. Please help teach our young people that what they do and say to one another off or online does make a difference.

Teens can use these tips to protect themselves online.

- Tell a trusted adult if you're being cyberbullied.
- If you know someone who's being a cyberbully tell her/him to knock it off. If they don't, report it.
- Contact host/site providers if inappropriate material is being posted on their site.
- Save all evidence if you're being bullied online. Don't delete without keeping a copy for yourself.
- Don't respond to rude messages.
- If someone angers you, wait, don't fire off a rude comeback. It'll only make things worse.
- Don't share personal information online.
- Protect your username and password. Don't share it with friends.
- Don't open anything from someone you don't know.
- Keep privacy settings on your computer. Secure your information.
- Choose your friends wisely.
- Only accept close friends on your social networking sites.
- Don't post anything online that you wouldn't mind your parents seeing.
- Most importantly, treat others as you want to be treated. Think before you click. Look at what your posting or uploading and ask "Would I want someone saying or putting that about me online?" If the answer is "No" then don't do it.

While the internet can be fun and super cool it comes with responsibility. Have fun with technology just take heed and exercise caution when using it. A joke is meant to be funny but not at the expense of another person's feelings. Young people joking is one click away from cyberbullying.

Viewpoint 4

Studies Show Cyberbullying Concerns Have Been Overstated

"Old-style face-to-face bullying is still the way most young people are victimized, even though it's cyber- bullying that seems to get all the headlines."

Sharon Jayson

In the following viewpoint, Sharon Jayson contends that traditional bullying is more common than cyberbullying. She maintains that reports of an increase in cyberbullying have been exaggerated. The author cites a survey showing that 18 percent of students in the United States have been verbally bul- lied, while only 5 percent have experienced cyberbullying. Although cyberbullying is a newer phenomenon, the author believes that traditional bullying poses more risk to students. She argues that traditional bully- ing is where schools and parents should put their focus. Jayson writes about behavior and relationships for *USA Today*.

AS YOU READ, CONSIDER THE FOLLOWING QUESTIONS:

1. According to the author, what percentage of US students have been cyberbullied?

2. Jayson states that what percentage of cyberbullied youth were also bullied in person?
3. According to the author, what is the number-one predictor of involvement in at-risk behavior among youth?

Old-style face-to-face bullying is still the way most young people are victimized, even though it's cyberbullying that seems to get all the headlines, an international bullying expert told psychology professionals Saturday [August 4, 2012].

Reports of a cyberbullying explosion over the past few years because of increasing use of mobile devices have been greatly exaggerated, says psychologist Dan Olweus of the University of Bergen in Bergen, Norway. He says his latest research, published this spring in the *European Journal of Developmental Psychology*, finds not many students report being bullied online at all.

"Contradicting these claims, it turns out that cyberbullying, when studied in proper context, is a low-prevalence phenomenon, which

Recent studies show that traditional face-to-face bullying is still more prevalent than cyberbullying.

has not increased over time and has not created many 'new' victims and bullies," the study finds.

Olweus says his research includes large-scale studies lasting four to five years; one includes 450,490 students in 1,349 schools in grades 3–12 conducted between 2007–10. Another study followed 9,000 students in grades 4–10 in 41 schools in Oslo from 2006-10.

Cyberbullying Is Not on the Rise

"There is very little scientific support to show that cyberbullying has increased over the past five to six years, and this form of bullying is actually a less frequent phenomenon," he says.

In the U.S. sample, 18% of students said they had been verbally bullied, while about 5% said they had been cyberbullied. About 10% said they had bullied others verbally and 3% said they had bullied others electronically. In the Norwegian sample, 11% of students reported being verbally bullied; 4% reported being the victim; 4% said they had verbally bullied others; and 1% said they had cyberbullied.

FAST FACT

According to a 2009 study of three thousand students, 38 percent of bullying victims felt vengeful, and 24 percent felt helpless.

His research also finds that 80%–90% of cyberbullied youth were also bullied verbally or physically in-person. Most cyberbullies—who spread false, embarrassing or hostile information online about a peer—also bullied in the traditional ways, he says.

Those who are bullied in any fashion often suffer from depression, poor self-esteem and anxiety and even have suicidal thoughts, Olweus says.

Other research about cyberbullying presented earlier at the American Psychological Association meeting also found less of a prevalence than many believe, largely because the studies haven't been uniform in their methods, experts say.

Findings "vary dramatically," says Ian Rivers, a professor of human development at Brunel University in London. He says there have been many studies about cyberbullying, going back to the early 2000s, but

Most Youth Have Not Been Bullied Online

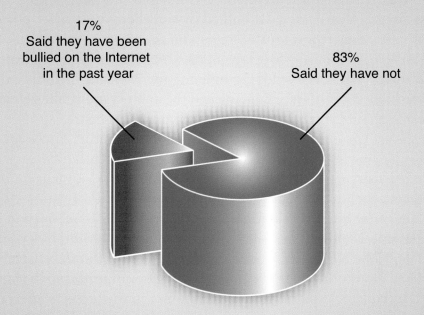

17%
Said they have been
bullied on the Internet
in the past year

83%
Said they have not

Note: Data from Michele Ybarra of Center for Innovative Public Health Research
from one study of 1,158 youths and another of 3,777 adolescents.

Taken from: Sharon Jayson, "Studies Show Cyberbullying Concerns Have Been Overstated," *USA Today*,
August 4, 2012.

"the one thing that is apparent is we weren't all looking at the same thing."

Two new, unpublished nationally representative studies do offer something more concrete. Researcher Michele Ybarra of the nonprofit Center for Innovative Public Health Research in San Clemente, Calif., has found that about 17% said they've been bullied on the Internet in the past year; 83% said they had not. One study was of 1,158 youths and the other of 3,777 adolescents.

Parental Monitoring Makes a Difference

Ybarra has also studied whether the bully was perceived to have more power than the victim—defined as being "bigger than you, had more friends, was more popular, or had more power than you in another way." That power issue does make a difference, her study finds.

"What we see is that those who say they were bullied by somebody with differential power were twice as likely to say they were really upset by it," Ybarra says. "If bullied by somebody with more power than them, they report greater impact on their lives as the result."

Psychologist Dorothy Espelage, of the University of Illinois-Urbana-Champaign, has been studying bullying for 18 years, including the old-fashioned face-to-face bullying and the online variety. She says her research about cyberbullying found the same 17% figure.

Espelage presented a study forthcoming in the journal *Psychology of Violence*, showing that parental monitoring makes a real difference in whether kids bully. Focusing on 1,023 middle school students in the Midwest, she found that "you should probably monitor your kids."

"They may be less likely to engage in perpetration in school and in perpetration online," Espelage says. "We know in criminology and sociology, the No. 1 predictor of any involvement in at-risk behavior is parental monitoring. It seems to be showing up confirmed in the face-to-face (bullying) and seems to be important in the online context."

Another study she co-authored that was also presented at the meeting found that those who are victimized are more likely to be perpetrators themselves. The researchers found that kids who were victimized face-to-face by peers at school were more likely to go online and engage in cyberbullying, to retaliate against what was happening at school.

Olweus, who has studied bullying for decades, says even though cyberbullying is getting a lot of attention, schools and parents should put the focus on countering traditional bullying.

> ## EVALUATING THE AUTHOR'S ARGUMENTS
>
> In this viewpoint, Sharon Jayson claims that traditional bullying occurs more often than cyberbullying. Who is more convincing, Jayson or Raychelle Cassada Lohmann, the author of the previous viewpoint? Why?

Cyberbullying Causes Teen Suicide

Felise Levine

"[Fifty] percent of suicides in youth are the result of bullying."

In the following viewpoint, Felise Levine argues that cyberbullying poses a deadly threat to youth. She cites research showing that 50 percent of suicides among youth are the result of bullying. The author details the harmful impacts of cyberbullying and explores why kids become bullies. In order to combat cyberbullying, Levine says that parents and schools must maintain a year-round awareness. Only through family accountability as well as school and neighborhood involvement, can the threat of cyberbullying and thus teen suicide be diminished, the author argues. Levine is a psychologist in La Jolla, California, and a past president of the San Diego Psychological Association.

AS YOU READ, CONSIDER THE FOLLOWING QUESTIONS:

1. According to the author, how many young people committed suicide in 2013?
2. What percentage of adolescents uses cell phones, according to Levine?
3. Girls of what ages have the greatest risk for bullying and being bullied, according to the author?

R ebecca Sedwick was almost 13 when she committed suicide after repeatedly receiving online messages telling her, "No one cares about u," "U deserve to die" and "Why don't u just kill yourself." She joins 4,000 other youths who have taken their lives this year [2013].

According to the Centers for Disease Control [and Prevention], suicide is the third-leading cause of death among young people. Although estimates of bully-related suicides vary widely, a Yale University study suggests that bully victims are up to 10 percent more likely to commit suicide than non-victims and a recent British study estimates that 50 percent of suicides in youth are the result of bullying.

Suicide Is the Third Leading Cause of Death Among Youth

Leading causes of deaths in the United States for ages 1–24, 2011

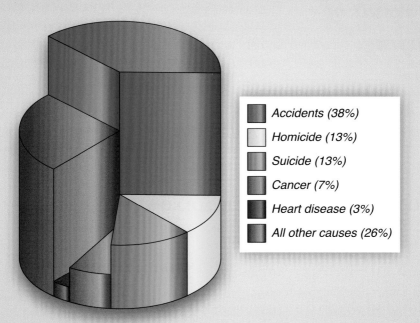

Accidents (38%)

Homicide (13%)

Suicide (13%)

Cancer (7%)

Heart disease (3%)

All other causes (26%)

Number of deaths = 39,213

Taken from: Arialdi M. Miniño, "Death in the United States, 2011," National Center for Health Statistics, NCHS Data Brief, no. 115, March 2013.

Approximately 85 percent of adolescents use cell phones and it is the cell phone that is the weapon of choice for cyber bullies. Under the cover of anonymity with easy access to the Internet, cyber bullies use texts, emails and social websites to harass, humiliate, spread rumors and threaten harmful things to kids who are less powerful. These messages quickly spread from youngster to youngster so that an organized campaign of destruction spirals out of control. With hateful messages and photos circulated on the Internet, there is little escape for the bullied child or teen.

FAST FACT

Approximately 4,600 young people between the ages of ten and twenty-four commit suicide each year in the United States, according to the Centers for Disease Control and Prevention.

Examining Why Kids Bully

Why do kids bully other kids? They want to gain more attention, power and popularity among their peers, and often have witnessed or been the victim of derogation or abuse themselves. Contrary to popular assumptions, bullies are often social and have good self-esteem, but they are more aggressive, break the rules and have low empathy for others.

Silent bystanders and kids who join the bullying are culpable as well. In middle school, girls between the ages of 10 and 14 pose the greatest risk for bullying and being bullied because this is the age when kids normally shift their emotional affiliations from the family to their peer group and emotional reactions related to hormonal shifts in the body can be intense. Friends one day become enemies the next in a rapid process of who is in and who is out. LBGT [lesbian, gay, bisexual, and transgender] youths also are at high risk for being bullied.

Are kids meaner today? Does the Internet cause cyber bullying? Researchers are just beginning to study whether cyber bullying is similar to other forms of bullying or whether it is an entirely different phenomena.

Numerous experts suggest that bullying is best addressed with a combination of individual and family accountability, and school and neighborhood involvement. If you are a parent, talk to your kids about the consequences of bullying. Set clear rules at home prohibiting bullying. Check your children's Internet use and ask them specifically if they know of kids who are bullied and whether they have been bullied or have bullied others.

Bullying Is a Serious Problem

Almost half of all elementary school and middle school kids in several research studies report that they have known of kids being bullied, have been bullied themselves or have been bullies. Take signs of depression (threats to kill self, low self-esteem, guilt, withdrawal, anger, somatic complaints), school anxiety and absences seriously and seek the help of a mental health professional. Contact administrators in your child's school and school district and don't accept comments like, "Kids will be kids, they'll outgrow it," or, "It's just a joke." Bullying is no joke. It is not normal behavior and bullies tend to become adults who bully. Children who are bullied have a high incidence of school absenteeism and suffer from a loss of security, safety and self-esteem that can last long-term.

San Diego Unified School District has clear and strict policies on bullying. They can be used as a model for other school districts. If you are a kid who has been a bystander speak up, comfort the kid who's been bullied and tell a trusted adult. Don't become part of the problem. If you have been bullied, get help from a trusted adult and seek the support of kids who don't bully.

EVALUATING THE AUTHOR'S ARGUMENTS

In this viewpoint, Felise Levine claims that cyberbullying is a deadly threat to youth and leads to teen suicide. Do you agree? Explain your answer.

Bullying Is Not on the Rise and It Does Not Lead to Suicide

Kelly McBride

"There is no scientific evidence that bully-ing causes suicide."

In the following viewpoint, Kelly McBride argues that bullying is not a direct cause of teen suicide. The author believes that the media are misinforming the public about bullying, and it is journalistically irresponsible to claim that bullying leads to suicide. Even in specific cases where a young person was bullied and committed suicide, McBride maintains that it is inaccurate to identify bullying as the sole cause of the suicide. Bullying and suicide are complex issues, McBride contends. She believes that the media should report the full story about the relationship between bullying and teen suicide and should help foster real change and avoid hysteria. McBride is the director of the Ethics Department and the Reporting, Writing, and Editing Department at the Poynter Institute, a Florida-based school of journalism.

AS YOU READ, CONSIDER THE FOLLOWING QUESTIONS:

1. According to the author, how many teenagers report being bullied in real life?
2. What is the reason that stories linking bullying and suicide gain such traction, in McBride's opinion?
3. McBride says that journalists owe what to the public regarding the link between cyberbullying and teen suicide?

Every other month or so a story about a child bullied until he or she commits suicide rises into our national consciousness. This month [October 2013] it's Rebecca Sedwick from Lakeland, Fla.

Before that it was Gabrielle Molina of Queens [New York]. And before that it was Asher Brown.

All suicides are tragic and complicated. And teen suicides are particularly devastating because as adults we recognize all that lost potential.

Yet, in perpetuating these stories, which are often little more than emotional linkbait, journalists are complicit in a gross oversimplification of a complicated phenomenon. In short, we're getting the facts wrong.

The common narrative goes like this: Mean kids, usually the most popular and powerful, single out and relentlessly bully a socially weaker classmate in a systemic and calculated way, which then drives the victim into a darkness where he or she sees no alternative other than committing suicide.

Research Does Not Show Bullying Causes Suicide

And yet experts—those who study suicide, teen behavior and the dynamics of cyber interactions of teens—all say that the facts are rarely that simple. And by repeating this inaccurate story over and over, journalists are harming the public's ability to understand the dynamics of both bullying and suicide.

People commit suicide because of mental illness. It is a treatable problem and preventable outcome. Bullying is defined as an ongoing pattern of intimidation by a child or teenager over others who have less power.

Yet when journalists (and law enforcement, talking heads and politicians) imply that teenage suicides are directly caused by bullying, we reinforce a false narrative that has no scientific support. In doing so, we miss opportunities to educate the public about the things we could be doing to reduce both bullying and suicide.

There is no scientific evidence that bullying causes suicide. None at all. Lots of teenagers get bullied (between 1 in 4 and 1 in 3 teenagers report being bullied in real life, fewer report being bullied online). Very few commit suicide. Among the people who commit suicide, researchers have no good data on how many of them have been bullied.

It is journalistically irresponsible to claim that bullying leads to suicide. Even in specific cases where a teenager or child was bullied and subsequently commits suicide, it's not accurate to imply the bullying was the direct and sole cause behind the suicide.

Reporters are often reacting to other misinformed authorities. For example, Polk County Sheriff Grady Judd explained to reporters that he arrested two girls (one 12, the other 14) in Sedwick's death, after seeing a callous social media post from one of the girls, "We can't leave her out there, who else is she going to torment? Who else is she going to harass? Who is the next person she verbally and mentally abuses and attacks?" While it's a great quote, it implies that this girl has the ability, through random meanness, to inspire others to commit suicide.

Misrepresenting the Bullying Narrative

"Everything we know about unsafe reporting is being done here—describing the method(s), the simplistic explanation (bullying = suicide), the narrative that bullies are the villains and the girl that died, the victim," Wylie Tene, the public relations manager for the American Foundation for Suicide Prevention, wrote in an email to

Common Pitfalls of Media Reports on Bullying

Common Pitfall	Why It Can Be Harmful
Overstating the problem. With so much discussion of bullying and an Internet rife with false information and misleading statistics, it can be difficult to keep the issue in perspective.	Creating the impression that bullying is a bigger problem than it is spreads misinformation, which in media reports raises many ethical and professional concerns. Some experts contend that reports depicting bullying as widespread and rapidly growing make youth and adults more likely to see it as common and less likely to try to stop it.
Stating or implying that bullying caused a suicide. The relationship between bullying and suicide is complex. Many media reports take short cuts, presenting bullying as the "cause" or "reason" for a suicide. The *facts* tell a different story.	Stories that say or insinuate that bullying caused a suicide can create a belief that suicide is a normal, even inevitable result of bullying. This may lead to "contagion"— additional deaths or cluster suicides that occur after heavy media coverage of the issue.
Oversimplifying. Journalists' efforts to simplify complex bullying issues for readers can be unintentionally misleading.	Reports that exclude nuances paint an inaccurate and incomplete picture of real-world bullying. This perpetuates myths and may lead parents, educators, and others to miss the bullying in front of them.
Using under-qualified sources. It can be difficult to identify true experts in bullying prevention, suicide, and other newsworthy topics. Spokespeople may have expertise in other areas, for example from working as educators, or from personal experience. But they can lack deep knowledge of these complex issues and lead you to misinform your audience.	Poor sources can introduce inaccuracies into reports, which readers and viewers may take as fact and share broadly. Misinformation perpetuates the problem.
Blaming/criminalizing those who bully. Many times youth who bully are not mentioned in media reports. Some reports paint a one-sided picture of bullying situations, quickly blaming those who bully or even portraying them as criminals. They also may blame the school.	Portraying those who bully in a harshly negative light shuts down healthy dialogue. Parents of youth who have exhibited some bullying behaviors may be unwilling to participate in prevention. Teachers, counselors, and others also can write them off as "no good."
Sensationalizing. Journalists must interest readers. Bullying incidents generally are not covered unless they involve serious injury, a death, many young people, or some other act that makes them newsworthy.	The emphasis on the most tragic results of bullying can encourage overprotective or anxious parenting, which studies have shown may harm children as they grow up.
Failing to include prevention information and resources. Research has not arrived at what definitely works to prevent bullying, but many media reports do not offer the public what is known.	The absence of information about effective prevention strategies for youth and parents implies that bullying has no solution, and does not help move toward one.

Taken from: "What to Avoid," US Department of Health and Human Services, www.StopBullying.gov.

me. "She (the victim) is almost portrayed as a hero. Her smiling pictures are now juxtaposed with the two girls' mug shots. Her parents are portrayed as doing everything right, and the other girls parents did everything wrong and are part of the problem. This may be all true, and it also may be more complicated."

Sheriff Judd has a record of grandstanding for the media. Yet, journalists are running with his narrative, despite the fact that experts on bullying and on suicide are suggesting that there has to be more to the story.

What's a journalist to do? Challenge the sheriff. Add more information to place his quotes in the appropriate context.

"Clearly allowing police to make statements about whether a bullying incident was the cause of the suicide is contrary to suicide reporting recommendations. He has no training to make this judgment," said Dan Romer, director of the Adolescent Communication Institute at the Annenberg Public Policy Center at the University of Pennsylvania. "It would have been good if those quotes had been put into context if they felt the need to include them. At this point, the stories are a lot of hearsay. So, it's a shame that the girls are being identified. But this sheriff is clearly on the warpath about this and he can get all the media attention he wants."

Remember the story of Phoebe Prince, a young Irish immigrant attending South Hadley High School near Boston? After she committed suicide in 2009, several of her classmates were charged with a variety of crimes. Slate writer Emily Bazelon went back and documented exactly what happened to Prince in the months leading up to her death.

Bazelon described how several of the students were active or complicit in acts of meanness, including veiled references to Prince on Facebook and yelling at Prince from a car. But those acts hardly amounted to the relentless campaign that authorities described when they announced the investigation and charges. Instead, Bazelon's story reveals a girl who was already experiencing mental illness when she arrived at South Hadley and stepped into an intricate and nuanced social reality that includes bad behavior as well as acts of compassion, sometimes by the same kids.

Bazelon has offered a cautionary approach to Sedwick's story as well.

A poster shows the support of friends and neighbors for the family of Gabrielle Molina, a twelve-year-old who killed herself after being bullied at school.

Adding Context to the Story

When faced with a story about bullying, especially one that involves teenage suicide, reporters can find resources designed to encourage reporting that informs and educates the public. StopBullying .gov recently published media guidelines designed to help journalists include research and resources in their stories that will add important context and avoid common pitfalls. (In 2012, I facilitated several meetings with a group of researchers and experts who advised the government on the creation of these guidelines.)

There are also helpful resources for journalists covering suicide.

While there are myriad mistakes that journalists make on these two issues, here are some of the most common ones:

• Perpetuating falsehoods through hyperbole or by confusing anecdotes with facts, such as stating that cyber-bullying is on the rise or is an epidemic.

- Implying that suicide is caused by a single factor, like a romantic breakup, a bad test score or being bullied.
- Suggesting, or allowing others to suggest, that bullying is criminal behavior.
- Allowing sources to reach beyond their anecdotal experience. Parents, teachers and school administrators are rarely qualified to describe research or trends.
- Equating all teenage aggression as bullying, when in fact there is a specific definition that involves sustained behavior and a power imbalance.
- Describing an act of suicide in vivid detail so that it creates a contagion effect among vulnerable populations.
- Glorifying a suicide victim in saintly or heroic terms, which could also contribute to the spread of suicides.
- Forgetting to link to local and national resources about suicide and bullying, including warning signs and strategies for intervention.

Journalists Should Deliver the Full Story

One reason these stories gain such traction is they are easy to sensationalize and they tap into a common narrative that children today are spinning out of control as a result of technology and popular culture. "It's every parent's worst nightmare," the news stories and opinion pieces tell us.

By contrast, [an October 15, 2013] *Christian Science Monitor* story seeks out experts and arms readers with research, facts and resources.

Reporters looking for more motivation to steer clear of the popular, yet erroneous narrative need only look at the way this story echoes through history. Whether it's the proliferation of cars, rock n' roll music on the radio, video games, cell phones, or social media, we find ways to demonize technology's impact on the young people who embrace it with such enthusiasm. Over time, we look back and marvel at our own hysteria.

Bullying and suicide are serious problems. Journalists owe the public more than they are delivering. We owe the public the science and research. We owe the public the knowable facts. We owe the public the nuanced context of individual cases.

Anything less contributes to a misinformed society, which robs communities of the ability to bring about meaningful change.

EVALUATING THE AUTHOR'S ARGUMENTS

In this viewpoint, Kelly McBride claims that bullying does not lead to teen suicide. Whose argument do you believe is more convincing, hers or Felise Levine's, the author of the previous viewpoint? Explain your answer.

Chapter 2

How Should Society Respond to Cyberbullying?

District Attorney Elizabeth Scheibel (at podium) and South Hadley, Massachusetts, police chief David LaBrie (left) announce charges brought against a number of teens for "unrelenting" bullying. Their fifteen-year-old victim, Phoebe Prince, killed herself in January 2010.

Cyberbullying Should Be Treated as a Crime

"We encourage people to urge their legislators to protect the lives of our youth by supporting [the criminalization of cyberbullying]."

Sofie Mattens and Dan Robbins

In the following viewpoint, Sofie Mattens and Dan Robbins argue that cyberbullying should be criminalized. The authors explore the harmful consequences of cyberbullying and detail tragic incidents that have resulted from bullying. Cyberbullying is a growing problem that can cause both physical and emotional pain, they argue. The authors also review how bullying disproportionally affects lesbian, gay, bisexual, and transgender (LGBT) youth and how a proposed law in Maine may help curb cyberbullying. The authors believe that making cyberbullying a criminal offense would protect victims and remove cyberbullies' wall of anonymity. At the time of writing, Mattens and Robbins were graduate students in social work at the University of Maine.

AS YOU READ, CONSIDER THE FOLLOWING QUESTIONS:

1. According to the authors, what do bullies use to make others feel ashamed of their differences?

2. What is a common element of many cases of bullying, according to the authors?
3. Mattens and Robbins claim that how many states include electronic harassment in bullying laws?

Most—if not all—of us have had an experience with bullying.

Bullies torment and discriminate against anybody based on age, race, religion, disability, sexual orientation, gender, family status, national origin and any other personal characteristic that identifies a person as a unique and special human being.

Bullying Has Tragic Consequences

Bullies use hurtful, mean language to make others feel ashamed of their differences instead of proud of them.

Both national and local media have given a lot of attention to tragic incidents in which bullying has had a vital role.

In 2010, Rutgers University student Tyler Clement killed himself by jumping off a bridge after his roommate broadcast a streaming video of Tyler sharing an intimate moment with another man.

In 2011, a Lewiston [Maine] high school student, Dax Catalano, was beaten severely in the mall after receiving violent threats on Facebook.

> **FAST FACT**
>
> North Carolina in 2012 became the first state to impose criminal penalties on students for cyberbullying.

Just this spring [2013], Kitty McGuire, a Maine middle school student from Troy, took her own life. Friends and relatives say bullying was at least partially to blame.

As society and technology advance, so does bullying. Whether it's through social networking sites, texts, emails or public posts, technology has created a new medium that allows bullies to intimidate or threaten a person while being protected by a wall of anonymity and distance.

This distance allows them to dodge any chance of being confronted with the direct consequences of their actions.

LGBT Teens Are Often Victims of Bullying

A common element in many cases of bullying is that the victims often are gay, lesbian, bisexual or transgender [LGBT]. According to recent research, 63 percent of homosexual students report that they have been bullied at some point in their lifetime. When all LGBT students are considered, the number rises to 72 percent.

Thirty-six percent of LGBT students report being cyberbullied, as compared with 20 percent of their non-LGBT peers.

Analysis of FBI data indicates that lesbian, gay, bisexual and trans-gendered citizens are among those most likely to be the target of violent hate crimes in the United States.

Many stories of bullying end in the victim's death, often by suicide. Other young people are injured, either physically or emotionally. How many other people need to get hurt or lose their lives after enduring constant attacks in their personal lives?

Cyberbullying Should Be a Criminal Offense

Currently, 47 states include electronic harassment in bullying laws, whereas only 16 states have specific laws regarding cyberbullying. All states, with the exception of Montana, require schools to have a policy regarding bullying; and in 43 states, schools levy punishment for the behavior.

Twelve states have implemented criminal sanctions against cyber-bullying and five states, including Maine, are proposing to make it a criminal offense.

Maine's L.D. 1233, An Act Regarding Cyberbullying, would make cyberbullying a Class E crime that can lead to a fine of $1,000 and six months in jail. When a person has two or more prior convictions and is bullying the same person or has presented with similar conduct in a different jurisdiction, it can become a Class C crime with a $5,000 fine and up to five years of prison.

Last year [2012], the Legislature enacted an anti-bullying law that required schools to create and implement anti-bullying policies in

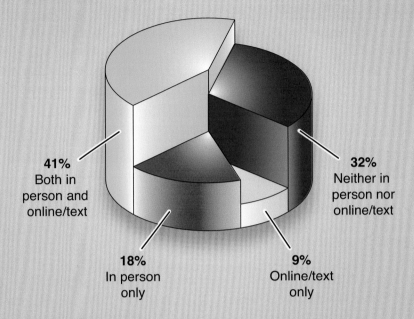

41%
Both in
person and
online/text

32%
Neither in
person nor
online/text

18%
In person
only

9%
Online/text
only

Taken from: "Out Online: The Experiences of Lesbian, Gay, Bisexual, and Transgender Youth on the Internet," Gay, Lesbian and Straight Education Network, 2013. http://glsen.org.

January. If L.D. 1233 becomes law, police enforcement will become new gatekeepers to monitor and put a stop to hurtful and damaging technology-based conduct, much of which occurs outside school property.

Our community cannot deny that harassment through technological devices is a growing issue to which an effective resolution has yet to be found. Progress is being made by increasing awareness and recognizing there is a problem. Schools are taking a stand by developing policies to increase awareness about, prevent and act on bullying behavior.

We believe that L.D. 1233 would help break down the wall of anonymity that protects cyberbullies and would help victims to put a stop to these cruel actions. This legislation takes the next step: making cyberbullying a criminal offense.

We encourage people to urge their legislators to protect the lives of our youth by supporting L.D. 1233.

EVALUATING THE AUTHORS' ARGUMENTS

In this viewpoint, Sofie Mattens and Dan Robbins maintain that cyberbullies should be held legally responsible for their actions. Do you support the criminalization of cyberbullying? Why or why not?

Cyberbullying Should Not Be Treated as a Crime

"Preventing cyber bullying is important, but so is finding more and better ways to mediate disputes between children."

Mike Riggs

In the following viewpoint, Mike Riggs argues that cyberbullying should not be criminalized. Law enforcement should not handle cyberbullying, he argues; that role belongs to parents. Riggs cites research showing that 66 percent of cyberbullying victims who turned to their parents for help were able to improve the situation. He believes that combating cyberbullying is important but that there are better methods than making the bullies into criminals. Riggs is the communications director for Families Against Mandatory Minimums and a former writer for Atlantic Media, *Reason*, the *Washington City Paper*, and the *Daily Caller*.

AS YOU READ, CONSIDER THE FOLLOWING QUESTIONS:
1. According to the author, has the rate of cyberbullying increased or declined since 2011?
2. Between 2011 and 2013, what was the increase in the number of cyberbullying victims who turned to their parents for help, as stated by Riggs?

There's a lot to be happy about in a newly released survey [2013] from MTV and the Associated Press about trends in "digital abuse" among young Americans. Cyber bullying among people aged 14–24 appears to have declined since 2011. While that's arguably great news, the most important finding in the survey is actually this: When respondents were asked how often they considered the possibility that what they say online or via text message could get them "in trouble with the police," 69 percent of respondents said they'd considered the possibility "only a little" or "never." Seventy-one percent of respondents had given little or no thought to the possibility that their wireless interactions could get them in trouble at school.

Those findings are especially troubling in light of the recent suicide of 12-year-old Rebecca Sedwick and the subsequent arrest of two of her alleged bullies, ages 12 and 14, in Lakeland, Florida. The two girls stand accused of harassing Sedwick online and in text messages so brutally that it prompted Sedwick to climb to the top of an abandoned building and jump to her death. The Polk County Sheriff's Department charged them with felony aggravated stalking after one of them posted on Facebook that she'd bullied Sedwick, knew that she had died, but didn't really care. Based on the poll results above, the question we have to ask is if Sedwick's alleged tormenters, who surely knew that they were being awful, also knew that what they were saying online could have criminal consequences IRL [in real life]. To put it more bluntly, should a 14-year-old and 12-year-old be criminally punished for doing something that was clearly terrible but not clearly criminal?

Parents, Not Law Enforcement, Should Handle Bullying

Incidentally, Sheriff Grady Judd, who ordered the arrests last week, said earlier this week that he doesn't think police should be involved in most cyber bullying cases:

Most Young People Don't Consider Risk of Getting in Trouble Online

How much have you thought about each of the following?

When you post things on a website, Facebook or Twitter page, or share them by text message:	Have thought about some or a lot	Have thought about only a little or never
That information could come back to hurt you later	54%	43%
That there's a risk you'll get in trouble with your parents because of it	34%	64%
That there's a risk you'll get in trouble with the police	29%	69%
That there's a risk you'll get in trouble with your school	27%	71%

Note: Numbers may not add to 100 percent due to rounding.

Taken from: "The Digital Abuse Study: A Survey from MTV and the Associated Press-NORC Center for Public Affairs Research," 2013, www.athinline.org.

I think law enforcement doesn't need to be involved in bullying. We don't need to make criminals out of kids doing what I call early-stage bullying. That's not good. We should be the last ones that are called. I can tell you this: the first line of defense is parents. Parents need to pay attention. They need to quit being their child's best friend and be their child's best parent. That's what they need to do. So it starts at home.

What I would like to see is a civil process and we'll have to think through this together whereby a school system can say, "I understand you're bullying and you've used this device. OK, we've got this anger management school, we've got this anti-bully school, and by the way, we get to hold your device until you've completed the school."

It would be great if we didn't need a new law for schools to effectively intervene in bullying, but more relevant is Judd's remark about the importance of parents. Between 2011–2013, the MTV-AP survey recorded a seven percentage point increase in the number of cyber bullying victims who turned to their parents for help. Of those who did so, 66 percent said it made the situation better. The only conflict mediation strategy that was more effective was when bullying victims changed their usernames and phone numbers, or closed their social media accounts altogether. According to Judd, Sedwick held onto her phone and social media accounts even after switching schools.

Cyberbullying Should Not Be a Criminal Offense

If it's unreasonable to deprive a bullying victim of the Internet in order to protect her (and let's go ahead and say that it probably is), should law enforcement officials everywhere be locking up her persistent bullies, Grady Judd-style? Criminologist Nadine Connell writes in *USA Today* that doing so won't fix anything:

FAST FACT

According to the American Osteopathic Association, 52 percent of parents with social-media-connected teens worry about their teens being cyberbullied.

[T]he use of criminal charges, as in the recent Florida case against two girls accused of bullying their 12-year-old classmate in the months before her suicide, does little to stem the tide of bullying or act as a deterrent for others. If history is any indication, the use of the criminal justice system as a punishment for bullying might not be beneficial to either victim or aggressor, especially because the youngest offenders fare poorly in our overburdened system.

Studies summarized by the National Research Council point to new developments in our understanding of the adolescent mind.

Adolescents lack the capacity for self-regulation in emotional situations, and young offenders cannot gauge future consequences in the same way adults can.

Bullying behavior falls into this category, as students are often reacting out of emotional frustration and a need to feel in control. The threat of punishment is often discounted due to the heightened emotion of the moment and sensitivity to more immediate interests, such as peer pressure.

If there's a retort to Connell, it's that teens theoretically *could be* dissuaded from cyber bullying if there was a strict enough punishment that teens all knew about. When a teenager commits murder, there's seldom a question of criminal intent or knowledge of the law. But think about what it would take to apply this standard to cyber bullying: We could create criminal penalties for teens being mean to each other on the Internet, but they'd also have to apply to non-digital bullying. The laws would also have to be overly broad in order to provide multiple opportunities for law enforcement intervention and guarantee prosecution, and we'd probably want them to apply in some

Many experts feel that a child's best defense against a serious problem such as cyberbullying is to talk to their parents.

way or another to parents, because how can you punish a 12-year-old without at least asking why his or her parent let things get this far?

With that broad net, we'd end up with the possibility of criminalizing bullies of every caliber—from the guy who called me a "faggot" after I picked the name Pierre on the first day of freshman French class, to cadres of pre-teens who call each other "skanks" on Facebook, to the really rabid and hardcore bullies who hounded Sedwick off a ledge—widening the school-to-prison pipeline considerably. Would it reduce bullying? Maybe. But it could also play out like the "zero tolerance" movement that was meant to prevent weapons in schools: such policies have resulted in children being punished for bringing a Lego toy gun to daycare and chewing a breakfast pastry into the shape of a pistol.

Preventing cyber bullying is important, but so is finding more and better ways to mediate disputes between children without involving the criminal justice system.

EVALUATING THE AUTHOR'S ARGUMENTS

In this viewpoint, Mike Riggs contends that criminalizing bullies will not prevent cyberbullying. Who do you believe is more convincing, Riggs or Sofie Mattens and Dan Robbins, the authors of the previous viewpoint? Explain your answer.

Cyberbullying Laws Must Not Threaten Free Speech

Scott Forsyth

"The local law prohibits speech protected by the First Amendment and is impermissibly vague."

In the following viewpoint, Scott Forsyth argues that cyberbullying laws often violate the First Amendment but must not do so. He discusses a 2012 law passed by the Monroe County Legislature in New York that makes cyberbullying against any minor a misdemeanor. The author examines the details of the law and concludes that it is too vague in its characterization of behaviors that constitute bullying. The author argues that the law should be repealed. Fighting against cyberbullying must not come at the cost of violating the First Amendment, Forsyth maintains. Forsyth is a partner at the Forsyth and Forsyth law firm in Rochester, New York, and counsel to the New York Civil Liberties Union.

AS YOU READ, CONSIDER THE FOLLOWING QUESTIONS:
1. According to the author, cyberbullying against a minor will result in what punishment now that the Monroe County law has passed?
2. Forsyth claims that the US Supreme Court has set what limits on the criminalization of speech?

Fighting cyber bullying directed at minors is up there with motherhood and apple pie these days. Last week [June 2012], the Monroe County [New York] Legislature passed a local law "Prohibiting Cyber Bullying in Monroe County" by the margin of 22 to 5. This week the New York State Legislature passed a broader law on the subject.

Who would speak out against these efforts? The New York Civil Liberties Union [NYCLU] for one.

The NYCLU applauded the county legislature's desire to do something about bullying but decried its approach—criminalizing behavior after the harm has been done. In addition, the NYCLU pointed out the local law prohibits speech protected by the First Amendment and is impermissibly vague. As is often the case, the devil is in the details of the law.

FAST FACT

A September 2012 survey by the Pew Research Center found that 95 percent of teens aged twelve to seventeen were online.

The Law Casts a Wide Net

The law makes "cyber bullying against any minor in Monroe County" a misdemeanor. Conviction may result in a fine "and/or up to one year's imprisonment."

Cyber bullying is "engaging in a course of conduct or repeatedly committing acts of abusive behavior . . . by communication or causing a communication to be sent by mechanical or electronic means . . ." "with (the) intent to harass, annoy, threaten or place another in fear of personal injury."

"Acts of abusive behavior shall include, but not (be) limited to: taunting, threatening; intimidating; insulting; tormenting; humiliating . . ."

What jumps out immediately is the sweep of the law. Calling a minor a nerd or commenting on his or her virginity may be viewed

"Who would've thought Ms. Kent was following our tweets?"

"Who would've thought Ms. Kent was following our tweets?," cartoon by Martha Campbell, www.Cartoon Stock.com. Copyright © Martha Campbell. Reproduction rights obtainable from www.CartoonStock.com.

as insulting or humiliating. A person is guilty if he simply communicates "against" or about a minor with the intent to annoy or harass the minor. The communication need not be sent to the minor.

Fortunately, the Supreme Court has set limits on the criminalization of speech. Only four categories of speech can be punished: (1) fighting words, words "which by their very utterance inflict injury or tend to incite an immediate breach of peace," (2) incitement, statements "directed to inciting or producing imminent lawless action" and are likely to produce such action, (3) obscenity, and (4) true

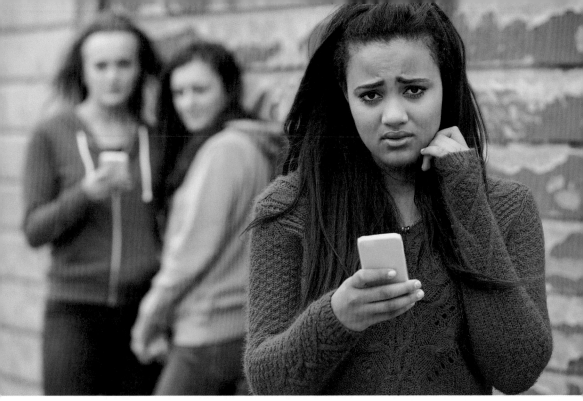

Some critics argue that sending upsetting or embarrassing texts are protected by the First Amendment, which does not criminalize annoying or humiliating language.

threats, "statements where the speaker means to communicate a serious expression and an intent to commit an unlawful violence."

Annoying and insulting speech does not fit any of these categories.

Protecting minors from potentially harmful speech is not a fifth exception. The Supreme Court rejected this argument when it invalidated the Communications Decency Act in 1997 and the Child Online Protection Act in 2002.

The Law Is Too Vague

The fact the county legislature intended to regulate electronic speech makes no difference to the First Amendment analysis. "(W)hatever the challenges of applying the Constitution to ever-advancing technology, the basic principles of freedom of speech and the press . . . do not vary when a new and different medium for communication appears," *Brown v. Entm't Merch's Ass'n,* 131 S. Ct. 2729, 2733 (2011).

Besides being overbroad, the law is too vague on its face. It employs a list of ambiguous and subjective terms, such as annoy, taunt and humiliate to define what is prohibited. It does not "give a person of ordinary intelligence fair notice (of what) conduct is forbidden." The need for notice is greatest when a law regulates speech, to prevent self-censorship.

The New York Legislature took a different and more proactive approach to cyber bullying. It saw the behavior as a failure of education and charged school districts with developing strategies to combat cyber bullying through lessons and monitoring student communications on and off campus. It did not criminalize the behavior.

However, in the rush to pass a law the state legislature selected vague and overbroad terminology also. It defined cyber bullying in part as conduct or an expression that "reasonably would be expected to cause . . . emotional harm to a student." An off-campus communication may be sanctioned if it is foreseeable that the communication "might reach" school property and it is foreseeable the communication may disrupt substantially the school environment.

The county legislature faulted the state for not acting on a critical issue. Now that the state has, it will be interesting to see if the county executive enforces the local law or if the legislature does the right thing and repeals the law. Most likely, the county executive and the legislature will do nothing. They have proven themselves to the voters, the First Amendment notwithstanding.

EVALUATING THE AUTHOR'S ARGUMENTS

In this viewpoint, Scott Forsyth asserts that the government cannot pass cyberbullying laws that violate the First Amendment. In your opinion, what is the best way to protect free expression and prevent cyberbullying?

Cyberbullying Laws Can Protect Children and Not Threaten Free Speech

Michael Meyerson

"The Maryland legislature ... passed ... a bill crafted to respect First Amendment principles while ensuring that parents will finally be able to protect their children."

In the following viewpoint, Michael Meyerson contends that cyberbullying laws can protect children from cyberbullying and yet not threaten free speech. The author highlights Grace's Law, a bill passed by the Maryland legislature in 2013. The law prohibits using electronic communications to repeatedly inflict distress on a minor or threaten a minor with serious injury or death. The author supports the passage of the law and maintains that it will protect youth from cyberbullying. Meyerson is the Wilson H. Elkins Professor of Law and Piper and Marbury Faculty Fellow at the University of Baltimore School of Law. He is also the author of *Endowed by Our Creator: The Birth of Religious Freedom in America*.

Cellphones and the Internet have not only altered the way we communicate, they have changed the way we can injure one another. The telecommunications revolution has created the capability of causing far greater harm to children than the bullying many of us remember from when we were young. The omnipresent nature of the Internet means that there is no place for the child who is victimized to hide. Not even one's home is a safe haven when repeated, vicious attacks appear on Facebook and Twitter.

Prohibiting Cyberbullying Will Protect Children

In April 2012, a Howard County [Maryland] high school student, 15-year old Grace McComas, took her own life after enduring almost a year of cruel, unrelenting electronic torment. That tragedy served as a catalyst for those who recognize that the dangers posed by new communications technology require a new approach if we want to protect our children.

In our quest to prevent electronic assaults on children, however, it is critical that the timeless importance of freedom of speech be fully protected. Any attempt to prevent cyberbullying must ensure that the Internet remains free for full and unfettered public discussion.

FAST FACT

Girls are more likely than boys to report being cyberbullied, according to a Pew Research Center report.

Fortunately, it is possible to find a balance. Both houses of the Maryland legislature have passed, and sent to Gov. Martin O'Malley, a bill crafted to respect First Amendment principles while ensuring

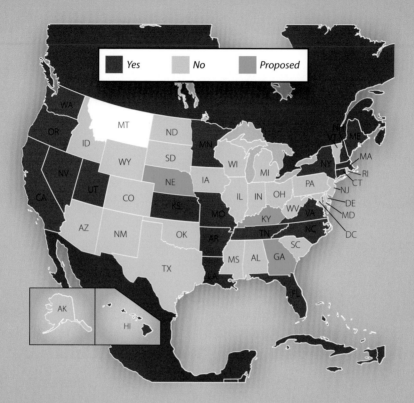

Note: Includes laws that actually include the terms "cyberbullying" or "cyber-bullying." This is compared to states that simply refer to electronic harassment or bullying using electronic means.

Taken from: Sameer Hinduja and Justin W. Patchin, "State Cyberbullying Laws: A Brief Review of State Cyberbullying Laws and Policies," Cyberbullying Research Center, April 2014. www.cyberbullying.us.

that parents will finally be able to protect their children. Appropriately named "Grace's Law," this bill, if signed, would prohibit anyone from repeatedly using electronic communications to threaten a minor with death or serious injury. It would also prohibit someone from repeatedly and maliciously using electronic communications to inflict serious emotional distress on a minor.

Examining Supreme Court Rulings on Abusive Speech

The Supreme Court has repeatedly held that threats of violence, such as those banned by Grace's Law, are outside the protection of the First Amendment. So called "true threats," in which a speaker communicates a serious expression of an intent to commit an act of violence against a particular individual, are simply not a part of the American marketplace of ideas. Intimidation, defined as directing a threat against others with the intent of placing them in fear of their life or safety, is viewed as abusive conduct and is also not shielded by the First Amendment.

Unlike "true threats," some speech that causes serious emotional distress has been found to be constitutionally protected. In 1988, the Supreme Court ruled that *Hustler* magazine could not be sued for a crude and nasty parody it had published of television evangelist Reverend Jerry Falwell. The court stated that in order for debate on public issues to be uninhibited, people who thrust themselves into the public limelight must be willing to subject themselves to "vehement, caustic, and sometimes unpleasantly sharp attacks."

In 2011, the court extended this protection for abusive speech to the Westboro Baptist Church, which had publicized its opposition to allowing homosexuals to serve in the military by picketing at the funeral of Matthew Snyder, a soldier from Carroll County (who was straight) who was killed in Iraq while on active duty. The church members carried signs that read "Thank God for Dead Soldiers" and "God Hates You." Despite the predictable emotional harm caused to Matthew's parents, the Supreme Court ruled that the pickets were protected by the First Amendment because they were part of a bona fide discussion of a matter of public concern.

The court recognized, though, that speech of a private matter concerning private individuals should be treated differently than the Westboro pickets and the Hustler advertisement. Protecting purely private people from the injuries caused by purely private speech, the court said, poses "no threat to the free and robust debate of public issues" and creates "no potential interference with a meaningful dialogue of ideas."

Protect Free Speech and Children

"Grace's Law" does not prevent or penalize the public discussion of matters of public concern. Its scope is limited to minors, the most vulnerable segment of our population. It has long been understood

The use of electronic communications to repeatedly inflict distress on a minor or threaten a minor with serious injury or death is illegal in Maryland.

that laws protecting children should be viewed with special solicitude. Moreover, the law would not penalize the random comment or even the occasional insult that is a part of daily life. Rather, the law's coverage is limited to those who deliberately engage in an ongoing course of conduct that is motivated by a proven desire to cause a child to suffer serious emotional distress.

Grace's Law is an important step in providing needed protection for the children of our state, while respecting and protecting the First Amendment rights of Maryland citizens.

EVALUATING THE AUTHOR'S ARGUMENTS

In this viewpoint, Michael Meyerson claims that laws can both prohibit cyberbullying and protect free speech. What is your opinion on the issue? Do you believe an effective cyberbullying law can still protect freedom of expression? Cite from the viewpoints in explaining your answer.

Should Parents Be Criminally Liable for Kids' Cyberbullying?

"I would support legislation that places legal responsibility on parents, making them liable for what the children do with the online access parents provide."

Mark O'Mara

In the following viewpoint, Mark O'Mara argues that parents should be held responsible for the online actions of their children. He believes that parents must understand that the technology they give their children can be used to break the law and cause harm. O'Mara believes that if parents are held liable for what their children do online, this will reduce cyberbullying. The author concludes that the only way to protect youth is to regulate social media and hold parents responsible for cyberbullying. O'Mara is a lawyer in Orlando, Florida, and a legal analyst for CNN, the Cable News Network.

AS YOU READ, CONSIDER THE FOLLOWING QUESTIONS:

1. According to the author, why should parents' ignorance of their children's actions online be criminal?
2. O'Mara says that the Internet is a fertile ground for whom?

3. According to the author, why has social media remained unregulated?

Two girls in Florida, 14 and 12, have been arrested and charged with aggravated stalking—cyberbullying.

They allegedly tormented a 12-year-old girl named Rebecca so relentlessly that last month [September 2013], Rebecca leapt to her death from a tower in an abandoned concrete plant.

The arrest came after the following post was made on the 14-year-old's Facebook account: "Yes IK I bullied REBECCA nd she killed herself but IDGAF." Polk County Sheriff Grady Judd said he would charge the parents if he could, but there were no "obvious charges" against them.

Before filing charges against the girls, Judd asked the parents to bring the girls in for questioning. They refused.

If a teenager makes Facebook posts about the suicide of the girl she allegedly bullied, the parents might argue that they have no effective way to monitor or curtail her online behavior. They could say they don't know what she's doing, and they don't care.

Parents Are Responsible for the Online Actions of Their Children

The question is this: Is ignorance and apathy about a child's cyberbullying criminal? Under our current laws, it looks like the answer is no.

But in a case such as this, should willful blindness or gross negligence be criminal? I think they should, and here's why: If a child kills someone while operating a parent's car, the parents can be held responsible.

If a child kills someone while using a parent's gun, the parent can be held responsible. If a child breaks the law using a computer or cell phone provided by the parent, how is that different?

Parents need to understand that the technology they give to their children can be used to break the law and inflict harm. Parents need to understand that allowing their children the privilege of going online comes with responsibility and liability.

A mother helps her daughter on a laptop. Some experts argue that parents should be held liable for their children's negative online behavior.

The father of the 14-year-old girl in this case spoke to CNN's Chris Cuomo and said he regularly checks his daughter's Facebook account. He said his daughter was asleep when the Facebook post was made, and he suspects the account was hacked. When asked about other online services used by the daughter, Kik and Ask.fm, the parents indicated they had not heard of them.

Most of today's parents would be astonished by their children's online behavior. But they shouldn't be. Just because today's parents didn't grow up with social media doesn't mean they can be forgiven for not knowing about it.

Legislation Can Make a Difference

The Internet is a portal to a boundless virtual world. It offers enormous opportunities for social interaction, and I'd suspect most tweens and teenagers would argue it is crucial to their socialization experience. If they're not online, they're missing out.

Use of Parental Controls Varies for Children of Different Ages

Have you ever used parental controls or other means of blocking, filtering, or monitoring your child's online activities?

Parents with online teens	50%
Parents with children ages 12–13	61%
Parents with children ages 14–17	45%

Taken from: Pew Internet and American Life Project, "Parents, Teens, and Online Privacy," Pew Research Center, November 14, 2012. www.pewinternet.org.

That means it is fertile grounds for those who wish to harass, antagonize or bully. And it's a place where they can inflict emotional injury in a detached, almost anonymous way—a coward's way.

If parents are not going to assume responsibility for their children's online access on their own—and it seems like the parents in this case are not—then I would support legislation that places legal responsibility on parents, making them liable for what the children do with the online access parents provide.

I am drafting a bill that would give Judd and other sheriffs the "obvious charges" needed to hold parents accountable. I do not think we should enact knee-jerk legislation because of a singular event, but this is not a singular event.

I'm thinking about the Steubenville rape case, where teenage boys felt it was OK to post photos showing abuse of a teenage girl online.

I'm thinking about the case of a former NFL player who discovered 300 teens were vandalizing his home because they were posting on social media while they did it. Where are the parents?

I understand there are substantial obstacles in the way of passing such legislation. Once upon a time, I worked for the Florida House Governmental Operations Committee, and I learned how to draft a bill that can pass constitutional muster and which addresses urgent matters in a balanced way.

While it is a straightforward process to hold a parent responsible when a child uses a dangerous object such as a gun, it's more difficult in the case of a nondangerous device such as a cell phone or a computer.

Moreover, holding a parent liable requires proof that they had knowledge of the activity, or at least were grossly negligent in their parental responsibilities, and we have to recognize that teenagers can find ways to avoid detection. In this context, a parent could be grossly negligent by having absolutely no supervision of a child's Internet presence (just like leaving a kid in a hot car, or playing on a busy street), or if a parent was notified of potential problems with Internet presence by a complaining parent or a school official or cop, and then failed to do anything to address it.

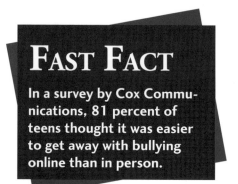

FAST FACT

In a survey by Cox Communications, 81 percent of teens thought it was easier to get away with bullying online than in person.

Finally, there are constitutional due-process concerns with holding a third party liable for criminal acts, especially when a statute already exists to hold the child criminally liable.

In the wake of this suicide, Judd has implored parents to take more responsibility for their children's online behavior. If parents won't adopt that responsibility, we need to hold their feet to the fire and insist they share liability, especially when their children's actions have life or death consequences.

Social Media Needs Regulation

Social media has entered the "Wild West" phase. It's been unregulated so far because it's fallen outside the view of our lawmakers. Nonetheless, we are seeing example after example of people using social media for nefarious purposes.

Cyberbullying is an undeniable problem, and we should not be satisfied with just asking kids to "toughen up and take it."

I believe that kids have a right to some sense of safety and security, and that is threatened by cyberbullying. It's up to parents to protect their kids, and if they don't know how to, maybe some legislation holding them liable if they don't will provide the needed motivation for them to get involved in their kids' online lives.

This issue is urgent and critical, and we need to act before we lose another child.

EVALUATING THE AUTHOR'S ARGUMENTS

In this viewpoint, Mark O'Mara claims that parents should be held legally responsible if their children engage in cyberbullying. Do you support legislation to punish the parents of cyberbullies? Why or why not?

Punished for Being a Parent of a Bully

Globe and Mail

> *"Parents of [a] bully could be sued for damages . . . without being directly at fault— except by being a parent.*

In the following viewpoint, the *Globe and Mail,* a major newspaper in Toronto, Canada, argues that holding parents legally responsible for their children's actions online will not combat cyberbullying. The newspaper highlights the Cyber-safety Act, which was passed in Nova Scotia, Canada, in 2013. The legislation holds parents liable in court if their children engage in cyberbullying. The newspaper questions the effectiveness of parents' spying on their children's online activity and contends that this type of legislation will not deter cyberbullying. Although cyberbullying is a serious issue, the newspaper believes that punishing parents will not solve the problem.

AS YOU READ, CONSIDER THE FOLLOWING QUESTIONS:
1. According to the author, what jurisdictions in Canada hold parents accountable for the wrongdoing of their children?
2. What does the Nova Scotia cyberbullying law require of parents, as stated by the *Globe and Mail*?
3. Why is parental "online hovering" impractical, according to the author?

Suppose a teenager bullies another teen online, and the victim goes on to commit suicide. In Nova Scotia, the parents of the bully could be sued for damages under the Cyber-safety Act, passed this summer in a hasty response to the cyberbullying and suicide of 17-year-old Rehtaeh Parsons of Cole Harbour. It's liability without being directly at fault—except by being a parent.

From here on in, parents could be deemed financially and by extension morally responsible for the suicide of a teenager they may never have met or been aware of.

Nova Scotia is not the only jurisdiction willing to hold parents accountable for the wrongdoing of their children. British Columbia, Manitoba and Ontario all have laws requiring parents to pay damages in cases of vandalism by their children. Those laws are based only partly on the idea that the parents have deeper pockets than their children. More important is the 20th-century notion that delinquent

A curious mother watches her daughter text on a mobile phone. Some argue it is unrealistic for parents to monitor every one of their kids' text messages or electronic postings.

parents raise delinquent children; deterrence depends on punishing the parents.

Or as the American Civil Liberties Union once said, it's the crime of having a child who commits a crime. That notion has wide currency in the United States. "There's virtually no defence—if you're the parent, you're liable [in civil court]," Eve Brank, a psychology and law professor at the University of Nebraska, says.

Some jurisdictions have been ridiculously punitive. Dermott, Ark., passed laws in the 1980s threatening parents with two days in an open-air stockade, and their pictures in the newspaper above the caption "Irresponsible Parent," if their children violated an 11 P.M. curfew. A 1985 Wisconsin law imposed fines of up to $10,000 on the parents and grandparents of unmarried minors who give birth. The purpose was to prevent teen pregnancy. (Guess what? It didn't work.) In Michigan in 2005, when a teenager set fires at a high school, the state made the parents criminally responsible, and fined them $700,000—without evidence they were at fault.

The Nova Scotia cyberbullying law is the only Canadian example that specifically requires parents to oversee online use or face liability in civil court. Parents are deemed guilty unless they can show that they exercised "reasonable supervision." But what is reasonable supervision in the context of children's online behaviour? The law doesn't say.

So where should parents turn to find out? Typically unhelpful is the Canadian Senate report *Cyberbullying Hurts,* subtitled *A Guide for Parents* and published December, 2012. It doesn't say much in a direct way about parents' responsibility to prevent their children from being bullies. "If your home is an environment of respect for others, of self-respect, of tolerance and open communication, it's more likely that your child will have the tools to not be caught up in cyberbullying—either as victims, as bullies or as bystanders who watch it happen and do nothing about it." Good stuff—but it has nothing to do with supervising computer use.

Even experts like Wayne MacKay, an esteemed Dalhousie University law professor who headed the province's Cyberbullying Task Force, aren't sure what parents should do, apart from parents offering a few words about good online citizenship.

There is some guidance—online—about what to do. Have the family computer in an open area. Ask your child how to use a social-

Parents Are Misguided About Their Teens' Internet Practices

Internet practice	Teens do	Parents aware
Clear browser history	53.3%	17.5%
Minimize browser when in view	45.9%	16.6%
Hide/delete inappropriate videos	18.9%	5.4%
Lied about behavior	22.9%	10.5%
Uses phone	21.3%	9.7%
Manipulate social media privacy settings to block parents	19.9%	8.1%
Utilize private browsing	19.5%	3.7%
Disable parental controls	12.8%	3.8%
Teens who have email addresses that their parents do not know about	14.7%	
Teens who have duplicate social media profiles that their parents do not know about	8.7%	

Taken from: McAfee, "The Digital Divide: How the Online Behavior of Teens Is Getting Past Parents," June 2012. www .mcafee.com.

networking site they use, and then peek at their page. Use an Internet filter to monitor what sites they use, and keep out certain ones.

But let's face it, none of these would do anything to stop online bullying—any more than a parent hanging out at the schoolyard would stop mean comments from being made.

For one thing, most young people either have laptops, or handheld devices, on which they can do their online bullying out of sight. For another, even a computer in open sight can't be truly monitored unless one acts as a constant sentry or demands complete access to one's child's private communications.

Are parents in Nova Scotia supposed to spy on their children's computer use?

It seems to us that would be bad parenting practice. Parents should not be in the business of guarding children against bad tendencies by hovering and nosing around computers, any more than they should listen in on phone calls. Children need and have a right to some privacy, within parameters. Parents in the Internet bullying age still need to show respect for their children.

Not that such hovering is practical, anyway. Should parents read the 100 or 200 communications their child might make in a night? (Heaven forbid they should have three or four children.) Parents have no way of knowing all the many social-media sites on which their children might spend some time. (Are they now expected to know?)

Many parents, perhaps most, are not nearly as computer-savvy as their offspring. Do they now have a legal responsibility in Nova Scotia to learn the ins and outs of Facebook, Twitter and 12 or 15 other sites?

Manitoba's experience with "reasonable supervision" may offer guidance. "Judges are really loath to find the parent responsible," says defence lawyer Josh Weinstein of Winnipeg, except where the parents knew their child was "a bull in a china shop and let them run loose." For Nova Scotia, a similar interpretation would mean lawsuits would succeed only where the parents knew their child had a history of online bullying and did nothing about it. But the law as written is not nearly so narrow.

Under the common law, parents could be held responsible only for negligence—leaving a gun or car where a child might do something terrible with it. Digital communication is incredibly powerful, and parents should try to help their children avoid being bullies—or bullied. But the state has no place trying to punish parents for doing so imperfectly.

Chapter 3

How Can Cyberbullying Be Prevented?

A student at a Maryland middle school holds up a magazine created by students in 2008 to help prevent bullying.

Viewpoint

1

Laws Can Prevent Cyberbullying

Catherine Dunne

"Involving the law makes someone take responsibility for tackling cyberbullying."

In the following viewpoint, Catherine Dunne argues that legislation can reduce the threat of cyberbullying among youth. The author details the impact of cyberbullying and maintains that society must find ways to protect children from this danger. Dunne believes that cyberbullying involves an absence of empathy for the hurt being inflicted on the victim. The only way to discourage cyberbullying, the author contends, is to hold the offenders legally responsible for their actions. Dunne is a former teacher and the author of *The Things We Know Now*.

AS YOU READ, CONSIDER THE FOLLOWING QUESTIONS:

1. According to the author, how many teenagers have been victims of cyberbullying?
2. What examples of cyberbullying does Dunne highlight?
3. According to Dunne, what percentage of young people turn to self-harm as a result of cyberbullying?

I was a teacher for 17 years, so I am no stranger to the cut and thrust of school life both in and outside the playground. But cyberbullying is something altogether different: this is the explosion of a new and insidious form of harassment, often amounting to psychological torture, and it drives teenagers to suicide.

Whilst researching my new novel, *The Things We Know Now*, I was shocked to learn of the exponential growth among young teenagers of cyberbullying. I began to dig deeper. As I dug, I learned that more than one in four young teenagers had been deliberately targeted, threatened or humiliated, either by another individual or a group, through the use of mobile phones or the internet. That's an awful lot of our children.

Teens Think Cyberbullying Rules Should Be Stricter

Percent of teens who agree with the following statements:

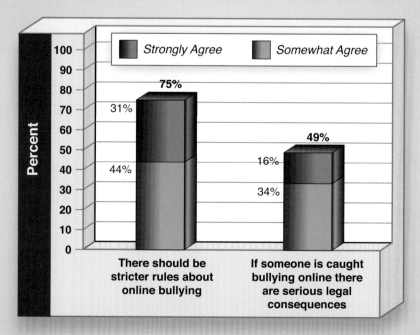

Taken from: Cox Communications, National Center for Missing and Exploited Children (NCMEC), and John Walsh, "Teen Online and Wireless Safety Survey: Cyberbullying, Sexting, and Parental Controls," May 2009. www.cox.com.

There Is No Escape from Cyberbullying

I learned that the abuse took many forms: text messages; hurtful comments left on social networking sites such as Little Gossip and Facebook; private images that had been Photoshopped and displayed for all to see. The most frightening thing, I learned, is the relentlessness of the bullies, and the fact that there is no escape from them.

Bullying is, of course, nothing new. It happened at the school that I attended, and it happened at the schools at which I taught in Ireland.

Now, though, it is no longer necessary to be in the bullies' physical presence in order to be bullied: instead, their presence is a constant one, 24-7, thanks to modern technology and young people's obsession with their mobile phones.

FAST FACT

CQ Researcher reports that 69 percent of adults believe that harassing someone over the Internet should be a punishable crime.

As young teachers in the 1980s, my cohort had some training in how to spot the signs of bullying among our pupils. How, though, can today's teachers spot bullying that goes on via a mobile phone hidden under a desk, or used late at night in the privacy of a youngster's bedroom? Yet the suffering inflicted by the cyber-bullies of this virtual world is itself all too real. Of the children and young people targeted, as many as five per cent turned to self-harm as a means of relief, according to the research I've studied. Three per cent had attempted suicide. Too many of that three per cent had been successful, youngsters such as 14-year-old Hannah Smith, who was found hanged in her bedroom last month [August 2013] after she received abusive messages on the social networking website Ask.fm. She is the fourth teenager in Britain and Ireland whose suicide has been linked to bullying "trolls" on that particular website. So what are we going to do about it?

The Secretary of State for Education [in the United Kingdom] has suggested in recent weeks that web bullying will not be solved by putting curbs on the internet, but by "fixing what's in people's hearts". Michael Gove said: "I think part of that comes from making sure that

A boy reads from a digital tablet at night while in bed. Cyberbullying can reach its victims anytime and anyplace via an electronic device, which means no place is safe for a victim.

we have the right behaviour and discipline policies in schools and that we teach our children the right values."

Legal Ramifications Will Fight Cyberbullying

It's a lovely notion to fix what's in people's hearts, but I'm not sure that it is a practical response. It's like so many aspects of human behaviour that inflict harm on other people: we shouldn't speed; we shouldn't drink alcohol before getting behind the wheel of a car; we shouldn't drive recklessly. But people do, every day, even while knowing in their hearts that others—and they themselves—might get hurt in the process. . . .

I am not advocating a ban on social media, not for a moment. . . . A good start would be to change the law regarding schools. This has been tried successfully in Canada where each school must have extremely robust policies, involving the whole school community and tackling the issue of cyberbullying head-on in so far as it affects any one of that school's pupils. This zero tolerance approach is not just encouraged. It is compulsory.

Cyberbullies Should Be Held Responsible for Their Actions

Involving the law makes someone take responsibility for tackling cyberbullying. As well as schools, how about the owners and operators of the websites implicated? They have huge responsibility in this, and yet in reality they do very little. They just want to make a profit.

How about starting with the moderators employed to outlaw cyberbullying on their sites? Set out their obligations in law, and then start prosecuting the owners of those websites who do not apply it. Why on earth should websites be allowed to carry comments that simply wouldn't be legal if made in the workplace? Why do we allow venom on the internet and believe ourselves powerless to stop it?

We are not. And where the law leads, the rest of society will follow. What lies at the heart of cyberbullying is an absence of empathy, an inability to feel, or to identify with, the hurt being inflicted on another. Once that lack of empathy is encouraged, sanctioned and protected by the cloak of anonymity that social media confers (even though every user can, ultimately, be traced, if there is a will and resources), we are confronted with the nasty, brutish sides of ourselves.

I'm not saying that social media is evil: of course it is not. Social media is a powerful tool of communication. But evil resides in the ways that some people choose to exploit it. . . .

It brings me back to that very uncomfortable truth about human nature: that the fear of being held accountable by law is often what motivates our good behaviour, not the common good, not altruism, not a finely-tuned moral compass. Take away that fear, as social media currently does, allow anonymous users to participate in mob rule, and the appalling effects are what we are seeing today—teenagers driven to suicide.

EVALUATING THE AUTHOR'S ARGUMENTS

In this viewpoint, Catherine Dunne claims that legal ramifications have the power to reduce cyberbullying. What is your opinion on cyberbullying legislation? Do you believe this is the most effective way to fight cyberbullying? Explain.

Viewpoint

2

Prevention, Not Tougher Punishment Key to Ending Cyberbullying

Marv Bernstein

"We now need to focus on ... prevention to stop cyberbullying before it occurs."

In the following viewpoint, Marv Bernstein maintains that tough laws will not eradicate cyberbullying. Bernstein says it is unrealistic to rely on the criminal justice system to combat cyberbullies and protect the victims. Instead, the author contends, the only way to fight cyberbullying is to focus on prevention. He believes that members of society have a collective responsibility to find effective prevention strategies and empower youth to protect themselves and others online. Bernstein is a lawyer, author, and the chief policy adviser for the United Nations International Children's Emergency Fund in Canada.

AS YOU READ, CONSIDER THE FOLLOWING QUESTIONS:

1. According to the author, what is a natural response to cyberbullying?
2. What did a Senate study on cyberbullying find about cyberbullying and tougher punishments, as stated by Bernstein?

3. Bernstein states that what outweighs potential legal consequences of cyberbullying for adolescents?

We are witnessing a growing number of tragedies from cyberbullying, most recently the tragic losses of Rehtaeh Parsons in Nova Scotia and Amanda Todd in B.C. [British Columbia].

A natural response is to search for a cure-all to stop victimization and loss of precious human life. Currently the federal government is considering closing perceived legal gaps and imposing tougher punishments against cyberbullies.

But Who Is a Cyberbully?

Any youth who passes on a defamatory remark or exploitative photo? In the cases of Amanda Todd and Rehtaeh Parsons, it seems dozens of young people appeared to have participated in the relentless torment. Is it realistic to rely on the courts and prisons to deal with all of them?

Where Are the Legal Gaps?

Contrary to what many believe, Canada has a strong set of legal and civil laws available for online bullying cases including laws against child pornography, the sexual exploitation of children, criminal harassment, uttering threats and intimidation. Civil remedies are also available including defamation, invasion of privacy and the intentional infliction of mental suffering. But these laws are not always enforced.

And last September the Supreme Court of Canada recognized the particular vulnerabilities and rights of children and ruled child-victims of cyber-bullying do not have to disclose their identity to pursue a civil case against an online bully.

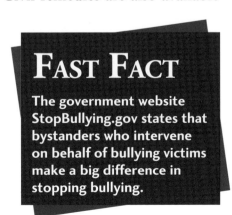

Fast Fact

The government website StopBullying.gov states that bystanders who intervene on behalf of bullying victims make a big difference in stopping bullying.

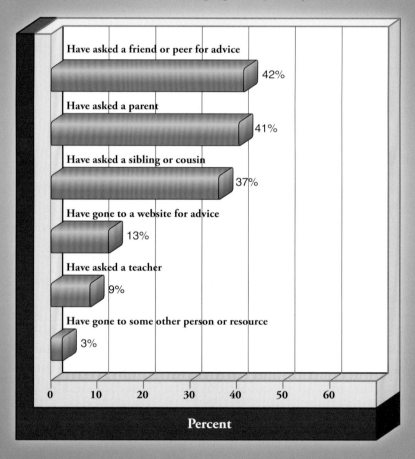

Teen Internet Users Go to Various Sources for Advice on Their Internet Privacy

Percent of teen Internet users who have used the following resources for advice on managing their privacy online:

Have asked a friend or peer for advice — 42%

Have asked a parent — 41%

Have asked a sibling or cousin — 37%

Have gone to a website for advice — 13%

Have asked a teacher — 9%

Have gone to some other person or resource — 3%

Percent

Taken from: Pew Internet and American Life Project, "Where Teens Seek Online Privacy Advice," Pew Research Center, August 15, 2013. www.pewinternet.org.

But laws aren't enough to save young lives.

A recent Senate study on cyber-bullying heard from dozens of Canadians of all ages and found no evidence that tougher punishments would end cyber-bullying or prevent it.

Since most bullies or those being bullied are children and youth, we would be punishing young people without any assurance that other youth would be discouraged from engaging in similar behaviour.

Youth are not only more impulsive because of their developmental stage, but they think less about the future. For adolescents, short term interests and the perceived rewards of offending are likely to outweigh potential legal consequences, which most young people view as remote possibilities.

Since Canada currently has sufficient criminal laws and civil remedies to address cyberbullying, we now need to focus on enforcement and more importantly prevention to stop cyberbullying before it occurs by improving education and coordination with the resources necessary.

So what are some of the solutions that trial and error have shown to be effective in preventing cyberbullying?

Education Is Critical

Children and youth have the ability and resiliency to protect themselves and others and to alter their own behaviour once they are effectively informed about risks.

This means empowering children at an early age to become good digital citizens and making informed and responsible choices when they use online media.

The Senate committee on cyberbullying has called for the federal government to coordinate a national anti-bullying strategy with provincial and territorial counterparts, promoting restorative justice programs (including mediation between victim and bully) and working with industry to make the Internet safer for children.

In UNICEF's recent report card on child well-being, Canadian children ranked 21st of 29 nations in incidence of bullying. Canada must examine what other countries with lower rates are doing right, such as Italy, Sweden and Spain so we can prevent more pain, loss and senseless death.

There is no quick fix to cyberbullying or the harm it has on our young people. But parents, teachers, social workers, health professionals, law enforcement, policy makers and the private sector all have a role to play in effective prevention.

With this assumption of greater collective responsibility by all of us to prevent cyberbullying from happening, these tragedies need not continue to affect the lives of so many young innocent victims.

EVALUATING THE AUTHOR'S ARGUMENTS

In this viewpoint, Marv Bernstein argues that enacting criminal laws will not prevent cyberbullying. Whose argument do you believe is more convincing, Bernstein's or Catherine Dunne's, the author of the previous viewpoint? Explain your answer.

Victim or Bully? Schools Need to Create More Choices

Jessie Klein

"Schools must take responsibility for transforming their bully societies into compassionate communities."

In the following viewpoint, Jessie Klein urges schools to protect their students from cyberbullying. Many school environments are like battlegrounds, Klein says, and students feel pressured to engage in bullying to avoid being victimized. The remedy for bullying, the author contends, is for schools to create a culture where students can trust one another. The author highlights the Zero Programme, an antibullying campaign in the Netherlands, which engages the entire school. Klein says the program has reduced bullying by 50 percent. While many are focused on legislation and punishment, Klein believes that the way to fight cyberbullying is for schools to engage in prevention. Klein is an associate professor of sociology and criminal justice at Adelphi University and the author of *The Bully Society: School Shootings and the Crisis of Bullying in America's Schools.*

AS YOU READ, CONSIDER THE FOLLOWING QUESTIONS:
1. According to the author, why are legislators in Albany and Suffolk County pushing new bills against cyberbullying?
2. What does Klein believe is the real antidote to bullying?
3. According to Klein, what is the term for suicides incited by bullying?

The January [2010] suicide of 15-year-old Phoebe Prince in Massachusetts reminds us yet again of how devastating bullying becomes for children and teens—from the severe depression and anxiety of millions of students across America to the spate of school shootings triggered by similar circumstances.

After each highly publicized tragedy there are calls to do something new. We have implemented zero tolerance policies and recess coaches, and states are passing legislation to amp up punishments for bullies and school administrators who do nothing to intervene. Legislators in both Albany and Suffolk County are pushing new bills after the suicide of 17-year-old Alexis Pilkington, of West Islip, last month [June 2010]— even though family members think cyberbullying was not a factor in her death.

FAST FACT

Fewer than half of the states with bullying laws discuss whether schools may intervene in cyberbullying, according to the *New York Times*.

And even though none of these after-the-fact interventions are likely to make much difference.

Schools Should Protect Students from Cyberbullying

Instead, schools must take responsibility for transforming their bully societies into compassionate communities in the first place. New laws that protect students from cyber- or real-time bullying will at best get rid of the most recent instigators in a particular place and time, but they do nothing to create a culture where students can trust one another, the real antidote to bullying.

Banners created as part of the Standup4change national program against bullying are displayed at a Scarsdale, New York, school. Antibullying school programs that engage the whole school population, and include continued follow-up and training, have realized greater success in lowering rates of bullying at schools than simply having a no-bullying policy.

While tempting, it's not worth spending time analyzing whether bullying is worse now than a generation ago. It was bad then, and it is bad now.

But it is important to recognize that kids respond to being bullied in more extreme ways today. In 2008, researchers at the Yale School of Medicine reviewed studies from 13 countries, and found a connection between being bullied and suicide in children. It's become common enough that the term "bullycide" has been coined for suicides incited by bullying.

Cyberbullying, Sexual Orientation, and Gender

Percent who have experienced cyberbullying at any time in their lives

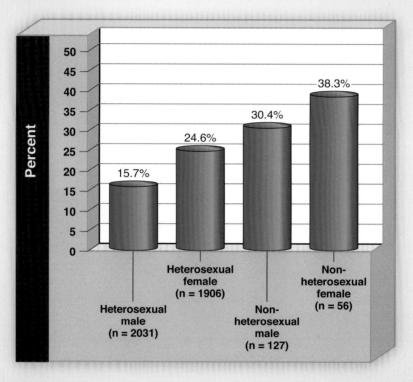

Taken from: Sameer Hinduja and Justin W. Patchin, "Cyberbullying Research Summary: Bullying, Cyberbullying, and Sexual Orientation," Cyberbullying Research Center. www.cyberbullying.us.

School Environments Foster Bullying

I've been studying school bullies and victims for 15 years. Many students have told me that they learned early that they had two choices in their school's battlegrounds: They could be the victim or the bully.

Boys in particular feel pressure to demonstrate that they are tough and masculine, and that they will use violence against other boys to prove themselves. They call other boys gay to trumpet their own attraction to girls. Gay bashing—against both gay and straight students—

becomes a norm in many schools. For the same reasons, boys also sexually harass girls.

For their part, girls feel pressure to prove that boys are attracted to them. Other girls seen as threatening this sought-after perception are often called sluts.

Phoebe, an Irish immigrant, was targeted because she had dated a popular senior football player in her first weeks at the school as a freshman. Other girls believed she was invading their territory and called her "Irish slut" and "whore." Her suicide recalls the brutal murder of Reena Virk, a dark-skinned girl who was killed in Canada in 1997 by girls who were angry that Reena had called some of the boys that the wealthier, white girls believed belonged to their exclusive social group.

Such racism and ethnic prejudice, mixed with gender violence, comes from values pervasive in the adult world. In fact, the bully society in schools is similar to the workplace bullying adults sometimes face. In the absence of alternative values, the cutthroat competition and discrimination prevalent in the larger society infiltrates schools and recreates similar power plays among children.

Students desperately want authentic friendships and connections. They find, though, that in school, their relationships are largely instrumental—students trade each other's secrets as information capital; they exploit their sexual interactions to try to become popular; and they compromise their former values to be accepted.

Where students look for friendship, intimacy and self-acceptance, they instead are tutored to mistrust. Why wouldn't they? Punishment for going against the expectations of those students perceived as popular may well land them at the bottom of their school's hierarchy and render them a target of relentless abuse.

Schools Should Create Supportive Environments

Yes, a recess coach—a measure being tried now in many parts of the country—might help prevent harassment from taking place on the playground. But it does little to teach students how to relate to one another in deeper, more fulfilling ways. Instead, students are likely to get the message that they have to be civil to one another in this particular place. The abuse then moves elsewhere: hallways, lunchrooms, buses, and MySpace and Facebook pages.

Parents and schools need to encourage students not just to tolerate differences, but to appreciate them. Girls and boys need to know that they can be who they are—academic or athletic, gay or straight, sexually active or abstinent, of any race or ethnicity—and be accepted by others in schools, and that other students and faculty care about them, regardless of the information they have about other students or the type or frequency of their sexuality.

This is a lot harder to do than simply passing new legislation.

The Netherlands national Zero Programme (as distinct from "zero tolerance" policies here), started in 2003, insists that all parties in schools are involved in a no-bully campaign "to create a broad base of support." It's not just a top-down anti-bullying policy, but a program that engages and involves the whole school. This program and the earlier Nordic version, the five-track method (help for the bully, the victim, the bystander, teachers and parents), has helped reduce school bullying by as much as 50 percent.

These programs succeed because the schools commit to training all school faculty, and to continuing the program's work after it formally ends. Lack of continuity undermines many of the approaches in the United States: Students here lament that successful models like "Challenge Day" help for a couple of weeks, but after they're dropped, everyone goes back to "normal."

One successful U.S. program is at Robert C. Murphy Junior High School in Stony Brook. The Get a Voice Project was started in 2002 by art teacher Laurie Mandel. Through professional development for a core team of adults in the school community, Mandel and her collaborators train faculty to create a more positive, respectful culture.

The program has reduced the number of incidents reported to the principal's office, and the students have significant transformations. "I spoke up, and that person listened. I made a difference," the students often say, with some surprise. "On their own, they won't stand up and say something," Mandel explains. So the program tries to enable them to "use voices of courage and leadership." Students come to trust that if they see something happening and speak up, someone else will speak up, too.

If we replicate programs like the Get a Voice Project and the Zero Programme, and help students appreciate themselves and one another, the United States will become a leader in eradicating bullying rather than the country that boasts the most school shootings and bullycides.

It's a school's responsibility to create supportive and empathetic environments where students can learn and thrive.

EVALUATING THE AUTHOR'S ARGUMENTS

In this viewpoint, Jessie Klein claims that schools are liable for creating environments that foster cyberbullying. Do you agree that schools should be held responsible for cyberbullying? Why or why not?

Parents Should Be Responsible for Preventing Cyberbullying

Gabriella Fuller

"Parent-to-child mentoring and online monitoring are the only real answers to the dilemma of virtual harassment and antagonization."

In the following viewpoint, Gabriella Fuller argues that the solution to combating cyberbullying is parental involvement. The author maintains that the risks of cyberbullying are too high for parents not to be informed about their child's activity online. Antibullying programs have the right intentions, Fuller says, but the most important influence on children is their parents. Parental involvement and online monitoring are the most effective methods to reduce cyberbullying, Fuller concludes. Fuller is a writer for Liberty University's *Liberty Champion* newspaper.

AS YOU READ, CONSIDER THE FOLLOWING QUESTIONS:

1. What have Kaitlyn Roman and Guadalupe Shaw been charged with, according to the author?
2. What percentage of teens use the Internet, according to Fuller?
3. According to the author, what trumps privacy and friendship among parents and their children?

A mother checks in on her child working at a computer. It is important for parents to take responsibility for educating their children on—as well as monitor—safe and appropriate online behavior.

"Sticks and stones may break my bones, but words will never hurt me."

Though we have all most likely said this catchy rhyme, the words could not be further from the truth. Words do actually hurt. And, as the nation has come to find following the death of 12-year-old Rebecca Ann Sedwick, words can kill.

Now, a month after the Sept. 10 [2013] death of young Sedwick, cyberbullying has become a topic to add not only to our dictionaries, but potentially to our laws.

Actions Have Consequences

According to authorities, Sedwick died jumping from a third-story cement plant structure after having been bullied verbally and physically. The primary perpetrators, 12-year-old Kaitlyn Roman and 14-year-old Guadalupe Shaw, have been arrested in the death of their fellow classmate and charged with aggravated stalking.

Polk County Sheriff Grady Judd was responsible for the arrest of the two girls. He later told CBS News that what the two girls did to Sedwick was "criminal because they terrorized her."

I could not agree more. Adolescent or not, actions have consequences.

Facebook posts from the bullies included statements such as "you should die, you should drink bleach and die." Shaw posted that "no one will ever know the truth" because Sedwick "went to hell" and wrote "yes IK I bullied REBECCA nd she killed herself but IDGAF."

The initials mean, "I don't give a (expletive)."

Judd has remained outspoken about his decision.

"She forced this arrest," Judd said after Shaw's shocking posts. "This went further than bullying. This was stalking. Interventions were tried by the school and by the victim's mom to no avail. And that's why we made felony criminal charges, because if this can't be taken care of at home, certainly, the system has an answer."

Where Were the Parents?

According to experts from the upcoming trial, this is the first time that stalking charges have been issued in relation to teen bullying. And though the arrests have certainly brought light to the gravity of bullying, these are only the first steps in the effort to resolve the problem of bullying.

Here is my question: where were the parents?

According to Judd, the parents involved in the case have remained uncooperative, arguing that there is no effective way to monitor or curtail online behavior. In essence, not only did they not know what their children were doing, but they also either did not care or were incapable of taking care of the situation.

Are ignorance and apathy a good enough excuse? According to parental liability laws, in any other case, negligence of a child would

Who Should Be Responsible for Bullying

Percent of responses from adults to the question: "Who should be responsible in dealing with bullying?"

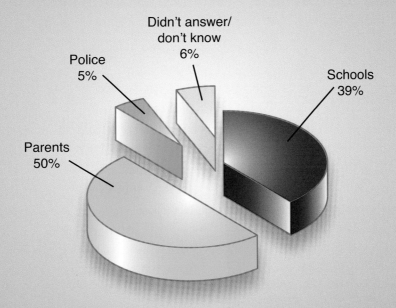

Police 5%

Didn't answer/ don't know 6%

Schools 39%

Parents 50%

Note: Data from "Most Adults Say Physical Bullying, Cyber Bullying Are Equally Dangerous," Rasmussen Reports, October 2010.

Taken from: Thomas J. Billitteri, "Preventing Bullying," *CQ Researcher*, vol. 20, no. 43, December 10, 2010.

be criminal. If a child kills someone while operating a parent's car, the parents can be held responsible. If a child kills someone with a parent's gun, the parents can be held responsible.

So why, in this case, is operating a cell phone or computer given by a parent any different?

Parents need to realize that allowing children to access the Internet comes with incredible responsibility—and liability. Technology is a powerful tool, and as we have seen, it can be used to inflict harm. Just because the current generation of parents did not grow up with social media does not mean they are excused from educating themselves about it—even if for nothing else than for their children.

According to a study by the Pew Research Center, 78 percent of teens now have cell phones. Ninety-five percent of teens use the Internet, and 93 percent of teens have access to a computer at home.

Parental Involvement Prevents Cyberbullying

The risks are too high not to be informed about social media and about a child's life online. More than cyberbullying programs or school initiatives, children need parents. First and foremost, a parent has a responsibility to raise and to guard. In cases like these, safety trumps privacy and parenting trumps friendship.

Though anti-bullying programs have the right intentions, children will most model what they see at home. Parent-to-child mentoring and online monitoring are the only real answers to the dilemma of virtual harassment and antagonization.

Emotional injury is as real as physical injury. Children need to learn that, although they can bully online in a detached, almost anonymous way, there will always be repercussions. As Proverbs 18:21 warns, "Death and life are in the power of the tongue." Our words and our actions have life and death consequences.

FAST FACT

According to the government website StopBullying .gov, studies have shown that adults can help prevent bullying by talking to their children about it.

It is time for parents to be parents again and to protect their children, to get involved in their lives and to recognize there is a need for regulation in a platform as boundless as the virtual world.

Regardless of what the courts decide for Roman and Shaw, the girls will carry the tragedy that their words caused for the rest of their lives. Whether we believe it or not, our words do have power. Jesus himself warned of this in Matthew 12:36-37.

"I tell you, on the day of judgment people will give account for every careless word they speak, for by your words you will be justified, and by your words you will be condemned," Jesus said.

To teens who believe their words are inconsequential: Think about that the next time temptation arises to cut someone down. And to parents who are uninvolved: Think about the poor influence you are having on your children by not talking to them about their media habits.

Every careless word. There are no rewinds or take backs. And though forgiveness can be given, the harm that is inflicted is permanent. Think before you speak. Think before you post.

EVALUATING THE AUTHOR'S ARGUMENTS

In this viewpoint, Gabriella Fuller claims that parental involvement is the key to cyberbullying prevention. Do you think an increase in parental monitoring would reduce cyberbullying? Explain your answer.

Viewpoint 5

Empowering Children Can Prevent Cyberbullying

Southwest Times Record

"It's not always easy to stand up to a bully, but when they do, they not only empower the victim, they empower themselves."

In the following viewpoint, the *Southwest Times Record* argues that children have the ability to fight cyberbullying. It defines cyberbullying and details the damage that it has caused. The author believes that it is vital for adults to teach children about cybersafety and to empower them to stop cyberbullying by refusing to tolerate it. If children are taught to stand up for the victims, the newspaper maintains, this will take the power away from cyberbullies. The author concludes that empowering children to protect themselves online is the key to fighting cyberbullying.

AS YOU READ, CONSIDER THE FOLLOWING QUESTIONS:

1. How does StopBullying.gov define cyberbullying, according to the author?
2. What makes cyberbullying so insidious, as described by the *Southwest Times Record*?
3. According to the author, what are the increased risks for students who are victims of cyberbullying?

It's hard to describe the problem of cyberbullying with numbers. Because the definition has a little elasticity to it, because the events probably are underreported significantly, because the offense evolves as fast as technology and because it can be pretty close to anonymous, we can't say for sure if it's one in three children who are victims or three in four.

But we know there's a lot of it out there, and we know it's damaging good kids.

The good news is that we can stop it—or rather, our children can stop it.

Defining Cyberbullying

Cyberbullying is using electronic technology—usually a phone or computer—to harass, threaten, embarrass or target another person, according to StopBullying.gov. By definition, it involves minors. When adults perform similar acts they may be guilty of cyberstalking or cyber-harassment.

It can include everything from mean or harsh statements on someone's Facebook page ("I hate you. Everybody hates you.") to hacking someone's social media accounts or creating fake accounts in someone else's name. It can include posting someone else's personal information or photos or videos to hurt or embarrass someone. It can be setting up a website to invite people to vote for the ugliest kid in school.

A sarcastic comment or a mean joke might or might not be cyberbullying: It can be hard to recognize someone's tone in a text message. But a pattern of cruelty is not accidental.

What makes cyberbullying so insidious is that it can take place 24 hours a day, seven days a week. A girl alone in her bedroom at midnight can be a victim of cyberbullying; there is no respite.

FAST FACT

More than nine in ten teens who asked for advice about cyberbullying said the advice they got was good, according to a study by the Pew Research Center.

Students who are victims of cyberbullying are at increased risk for anxiety, depression and other stress-related disorders. They are more likely to use alcohol or drugs, to skip school, to have low self-esteem, to get poor grades. They have more health problems, and they may try suicide, according to StopCyberbullying.org.

Children Have the Power to Stop Bullying

Cyberbullies like the notoriety and the power they get from the people they bully, but they get even more from the people who watch without intervening and from those who join in.

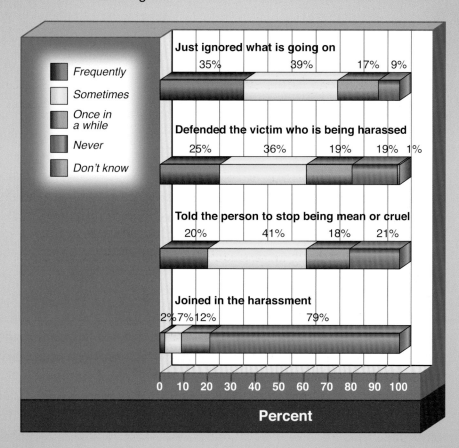

How Teens React to Mean Behavior Online

Percent of media-using teens who have seen others be mean or cruel

Legend:
- Frequently
- Sometimes
- Once in a while
- Never
- Don't know

Just ignored what is going on
35% 39% 17% 9%

Defended the victim who is being harassed
25% 36% 19% 19% 1%

Told the person to stop being mean or cruel
20% 41% 18% 21%

Joined in the harassment
2% 7% 12% 79%

0 10 20 30 40 50 60 70 80 90 100

Percent

Taken from: Pew Internet and American Life Project, "Teens, Kindness and Cruelty on Social Network Sites," Pew Research Center, November 9, 2011. www.pewinternet.org.

That's why it's so important that we teach our children they can stop bullies.

For peers, the most potent way to stop a cyberbully—or any bully—is to stand up for the intended victim. That takes power away from the bully.

Not everybody may be ready for that giant step the first time they observe bullying. We know that peer pressure is a mighty force with young people.

So there are other strategies that can help. Observers can talk to the victim later and offer to help that person speak to a trusted adult. Or a group of people can stand together to tell a bully to back down. At the very least, telling a sympathetic adult what happened can make a difference.

We also need to make sure our children know when it's time to involve the police.

Authorities should be alerted any time bullying includes threats of violence, pornography or sexually explicit messages or photos, photos or videos of a person taken in a place where privacy is expected, stalking or hate crimes.

Teaching Victims to Protect Themselves

Children who experience cyberbullying can take action to protect themselves. They should learn the three-point rule of cyber safety when they encounter bullying: Stop, block and tell.

When they first see something offensive, they should stop and calm down before acting. They should never respond and never forward anything offensive.

Then they should use social media safety centers to block the bully. Sometimes that's pretty easy, but sometimes they are going to need help from their trusted adults.

Children and the adults who love them should keep evidence of cyberbullying attacks. Before deleting anything, record the time and date, then take screenshots of the offensive material. Incidents can be reported to web hosts and cellphone providers.

A quote attributed to Martin Luther King Jr. reminds us, "In the end, we will remember not the words of our enemies but the silence of our friends."

HELP CENTER

Help Center Search

"bullying"

thing's Not
ing

ort Abuse or Policy
ations

s and Business
utions

ps, Games and
redits

afety Center

community Forum

FAQ Results

▶ **What should I do if I am being bullied or a Facebook?**
Facebook offers these tools to help you deal wit
seriousness of the situation:Unfriend — Only yo

▶ **What should I do if my teen is being atta**
Hopefully, bullying has been part of your ongo
the internet. The best protection against bullyi

▶ **What should I do if someone who is bei help?**
Here are a few things you can do if someone
report: Remind your friend to block the perso

▶ **What if my teen knows someone who**
Facebook doesn't tolerate bullying. Period. I
Standards and the Facebook Terms. We rem

▶ **How do I report abuse to Facebook?**
Pornography, hate speech, threats, graphic
Please note that we

Reputable social media sites have tools in place for users to report inappropriate messages and block the senders.

We need to teach our children from the first time they pick up a smart phone or sit down in front of a computer that they should never be silent about cyberbullying.

They have within their power the ability to stop bullying. By refusing to forward a mean email, by refusing to go to a cyberbullying website, by refusing to laugh or go along with a "joke," they can take the power and the fun right out of the bully.

We should teach our children that they have the power to stop cyberbullying by refusing to tolerate it. Showing support for the victim, showing concern for the feelings of others, and refusing to contribute to the mean games: These choices are theirs. It's not always easy to stand up to a bully, but when they do, they not only empower the victim, they empower themselves.

No bully can top that.

EVALUATING THE AUTHOR'S ARGUMENTS

In this viewpoint, the *Southwest Times Record* claims that adults must teach children that they have the power to stop bullying. What is your opinion on the issue? Do you believe this is an effective strategy to combat cyberbullying? Why or why not?

Bystanders Can Prevent Cyberbullying

"There has definitely not been enough attention paid to the role bystanders could play in preventing cyberbullying."

Joanna Finkelstein

In the following viewpoint, Joanna Finkelstein argues that bystanders play an important role in preventing cyberbullying. Although many prevention programs focus on the bullies and victims, the author believes the impact of bystanders has been lost. If bystanders remain quiet, cyberbullies interpret this as acceptance of their behavior, Finkelstein maintains. However, if bystanders take action, they have the power to protect victims and end the bullying. At the time of writing, Joanna Finkelstein was a computer science student at Pomona College in Claremont, California.

AS YOU READ, CONSIDER THE FOLLOWING QUESTIONS:

1. According to the author, the University of Toronto has found that how many middle and high school students have been bullied online?
2. Whom do antibullying campaigns focus on, in Finkelstein's opinion?
3. According to the author, what is "the bystander effect"?

On September 10, 2013, police found Rebecca Ann Sedwick's dead body at an abandoned cement factory in Lakeland, Florida. The day before, instead of taking the bus to school, Sedwick jumped off a tower and took her life at the age of 12. By the time of her death former classmates had been bullying her through social media for about a year with messages including "nobody cares about u," "i hate u," and "you seriously deserve to die."

The Cyberbullying Research Center defines cyberbullying as the "willful and repeated harm inflicted through the use of computers, cell phones, and other electronic devices." Researchers at the University of Toronto found that about half of 2,186 middle and high school students report having been bullied online.

Even after Sedwick's death, one tormenter continued the bullying publicly with "Yes ik [I know] I bullied REBECCA nd she killed her self but IDGAF [I don't give a f***] <3." Many people react to this story by blaming the two girls who sent the messages and their parents. However, people over-

look the fact that this post received 31 likes in just 15 hours. People usually ignore those who actually encourage the bully.

Focusing on the Bystanders

The current anti-bullying campaigns focus on the bully and the victim, not the bystanders. Crystal Lake Middle School, where Sedwick's bullying began, had an Anti-Bullying Week. The activities were "Walk in Someone Else's Shoes," "Wear White Day," "Band-Aids for Bullying," and "Anti-Bullying Pledges." The main messages were about sympathizing with the victim and understanding the importance of not being the bully. There were no directions for how bystanders could help.

Polk County Sheriff Grady Judd, who was involved in Sedwick's case said, "We don't want to criminalize this, nor do we want this to

When bystanders do nothing to stop a bullying situation, whether online or in person, it sends a message that bullying is acceptable. Antibullying programs should focus not only on the victim and the bully, but also on educating bystanders.

be a prediction for criminal action, but what we want to do is create a system, a method, an opportunity, so kids that are bullies, or kids that are victims of bullies are properly dealt with outside the criminal justice system," Again, he suggests the solution depends on the bullies and victims.

Facebook and other media sites are public; many people can view messages that others post. The bystander effect is the phenomenon where each individual observer is less likely to help a victim the more people are present. Thus, public media sites are breeding grounds for inaction.

A 2011 study by researchers at Ohio University, University of North Carolina, and University of Pennsylvania found that people are less likely to help someone if there is someone else present and if they strongly fear embarrassment. When a confederate of the study was present, participants were less likely to tell the experimenter she had ink on her face than when the participants were alone. Among the people that did help, those easily embarrassed were slower to help.

Strategies for Bystanders in Bullying Situations

Critical Choice Points 'NICE'	Social and Emotional Aspects of Learning Required	Discounting the Problem: Strategies from 'Say No to Bullying'
Notice that something is happening	Self-awareness Motivation	Its existence: "They were only having a bit of fun. Some people just can't take a joke."
Interpret if the situation is one in which help is needed and can be given	Empathy	Its significance: "It's not really that bad, is it— I mean there's much worse bullying where people get really hurt."
Choose a form of assistance	Managed feelings	Its solvability: "It's part and parcel of life—we just have to accept it as a normal part of growing up."
Engage with the problem	Social skills	Own capacity: "I don't like it but nothing I do is going to make a difference." "It's not really my business."

Taken from: Sue Ball, "Bystanders and Bullying: A Summary of Research for Anti-Bullying Week," Anti-Bullying Alliance. www.anti-bullyingalliance.org.uk.

Bystanders Can Fight Cyberbullying

Facebook and many other social networking sites have an easy way to report inappropriate behavior including cyberbullying. According to University of Toronto researchers, in one of four cases of cyberbullying there is a third party observer. It is clear that cyberbullying is very prevalent and that there are many bystanders that have the potential [to] make a change.

Although educating the bullies and victims might be helpful, there has definitely not been enough attention paid to the role bystanders could play in preventing cyberbullying.

If no one speaks out against the bully, the bystanders interpret the lack of response as an acceptance of the behavior. People make decisions on how to act based on the actions of others. Thus, the lack of resistance is contagious. Simultaneously there is a diffusion of responsibility because there are so many people on media sites and no one feels that it is her/his responsibility to speak up. This combination leads to great inaction by the observers.

Anti-cyberbullying campaigns should focus more on the bystanders. They should emphasize that no one should encourage or support the bully and that it is each individual's responsibility to intervene when she/he witnesses cyberbullying.

Helping a victim should be seen as something positive and empowering, not embarrassing. Further, it should be portrayed as what should be done and what is done.

Once one person helps a victim, the false consensus is destroyed and others are much more likely to also help the victim. Observers could calmly confront the bully, support the victim, or use an anonymous resource to report the bullying. These are simple and effective steps that are likely to spread and become even more powerful.

Even if the current campaigns are preventing some bullying, they are not eliminating it. In order to end bullying, the observers need to play a more prominent role. The current bystanders can become active fighters in stopping and preventing future cyberbullying.

EVALUATING THE AUTHOR'S ARGUMENTS

In this viewpoint, Joanna Finkelstein argues that campaigns against cyberbullying should turn their attention to the bystanders instead of just focusing on the bully and the victim. How do you view the role of bystanders and what type of impact do they play in fighting cyberbullying?

Facts About Cyberbullying

Editor's note: These facts can be used in reports to add credibility when making important points or claims.

The Role of Adults in Cyberbullying

According to the Pew Research Internet Project:

- Teens rely most heavily on parents for general advice on how to use the Internet responsibly and safely.
- Thirty-nine percent of parents with teens have connected to their teen on a social network site.
- Parents who have connected with their teen on a social network site are more likely to say they use parental controls to manage their teen's Internet access.

According to the American Osteopathic Association:

- Eighty-five percent of parents of thirteen- to seventeen-year-olds report that their teen has a social networking account.
- Of those, 52 percent worry their child will be bullied on such a site.
- One in six parents know their child has been bullied on a social networking site.
- Eighty-six percent of parents have joined a social network site or connected with their teens online in order to better monitor their teens' online interactions.

According to the Megan Meier Foundation:

- Students who said they were physically bullied reported their experiences to an adult 40 percent of the time in 2011, while cyberbullying victims notified an adult just 26 percent of the time.

According to Knowthenet:

- Two in three teens have experienced trolling or online bullying, yet only 17 percent of them would turn to parents as their first response, and only 1 percent would turn to teachers.

According to McAfee online security company:

- Steps parents take to keep their kids safe online include setting parental controls, which 49 percent of surveyed parents report doing.
- Forty-four percent of parents get their teens' e-mail and social network passwords as a monitoring precaution.
- Twenty-seven percent of parents report taking away computer or mobile devices as a step in monitoring or keeping their teens safe online.
- Twenty-three percent of parents surveyed say that they do not monitor their teens' online behaviors because the technology is too overwhelming for them.

Cyberbullies and Victims

According to the Cyberbullying Research Center:

- Females report being emotionally affected by cyberbullying more often than males.
- In a survey of 468 youth who had been cyberbullied, 39.6 percent of females reported being frustrated by it while only 27.5 percent of cyberbullied males did.
- Females surveyed also reported feeling angry (36 percent) and sad (25.2 percent) more often than males (24.3 percent and 17.9 percent, respectively).

According to Cox Communications Teen Online and Wireless Safety Survey:

- Cyberbullies spend an average of 38.4 hours per week online, compared with noncyberbullying teens, who are online for 26.8 hours.

According to the Pew Research Internet and American Life Project:

- Girls are more likely to be cyberbullying victims than are boys. Of online girls surveyed, 38 percent reported being cyberbullied, while only 26 percent of boys reported being so.
- Older teens are more likely to report harassment than younger teens. Survey results show that 16 percent of fifteen- to seventeen-year-olds say they have been threatened via e-mail, IM, or text message, while only 9 percent of twelve- to fourteen-year-olds report such threats.
- Teens who create online content are more likely to report being cyberbullied or harassed than are their peers. Content creators include those teens that blog, upload photos, share artwork, or help others build websites.
- Sixty-seven percent of surveyed teens think that bullying happens more offline than online.

Cyberbullying and Social Media

According to the Pew Research Internet and American Life Project:

- Facebook is by far the most commonly used site among teens who use social media, with 94 percent of these teens saying they had an account, in a 2012 survey. Twitter, the next most popular, was used by only 26 percent of teen social media users.
- In a 2011 survey, 69 percent of social-media-using teens said that peers are mostly kind to each other on social media; 20 percent thought they were mostly unkind, and 11 percent said that "it depends."
- Eighty-eight percent of teen social media users have witnessed other people be mean or cruel on social networking sites.

According to *Consumer Reports*:

- In 2010, 1 million youth were harassed, threatened, or cyberbullied in some way on Facebook.
- Of the 20 million minors who actively used Facebook in 2010, 7.5 million were under the age of thirteen and not supposed to be using the site.

According to McAfee:

- Ninety-three percent of teens who have witnessed cyberbullying online say that most of it happened on Facebook.
- Half of surveyed teens report having had a negative experience on social media.
- According to teens' survey responses, e-mail ranks as one of the safest online activities from cyberbullying. Only 6.37 percent of teens surveyed had seen cruel behavior on e-mail.

Organizations to Contact

The editors have compiled the following list of organizations concerned with the issues debated in this book. The descriptions are derived from materials provided by the organizations. All have publications or information available for interested readers. The list was compiled on the date of publication of the present volume; the information provided here may change. Be aware that many organizations take several weeks or longer to respond to inquiries, so allow as much time as possible for the receipt of requested materials.

American Psychological Association (APA)
750 First Street, NE
Washington, DC 20002-4242
(800) 374-2721
e-mail: public.affairs@apa.org
website: www.apa.org

The APA is the primary scientific and professional psychologists' organization in the United States. Its official position is that all forms of bullying exert short- and long-term harmful psychological effects on both bullies and their victims. The APA's available resources include the *APA Resolution on Bullying Among Children and Youth* (supporting H.R. 1589, the Bullying and Gang Reduction for Improved Education Act of 2009). The APA website offers links to a research round-up, bullying prevention programs around the world, and a Getting Help section for adolescents dealing with bullying issues.

American School Counselor Association (ASCA)
1101 King Street, Suite 625
Alexandria, VA 22314
(703) 683-2722; toll-free: (800) 306-4722 • fax: (703) 683-1619
website: www.schoolcounselor.org

ASCA sponsors workshops such as Bullying and What to Do About It and publishes the bimonthly magazine *ASCA School Counselor*. Free online resources include the articles "The Buzz on Bullying" and

"Appropriate Use of the Internet." The association's online bookstore offers titles aimed at young people, such as *Cool, Calm, and Confident: A Workbook to Help Kids Learn Assertiveness Skills;* antibullying posters, banners, and bulletin boards; and sample lesson plans for school-based antibullying programs.

Beatbullying
Units 1 & 4, Belvedere Road
London SE19 2AT
United Kingdom
+44 (0)208 771 3377
e-mail: admin@beatbullying.org
website: www.beatbullying.org

This organization provides an online social networking service that offers advice to those affected by cyberbullying. Victims of cyberbullying use the site to contact other teens who have been trained to offer advice and support. Beatbullying counselors are on call to take appropriate action to protect individuals from further attacks.

Center for Safe and Responsible Internet Use
474 W. Twenty-Ninth Ave.
Eugene, OR 97405
(541) 556-1145
e-mail: nwillard@csriu.org
website: www.cyberbully.org

The center was founded in 2002 by Nancy Willard, an authority on managing student Internet use in schools and the author of *Cyberbullying and Cyberthreats: Responding to the Challenge of Online Social Aggression, Threats, and Distress.* In addition to briefs and guides for educators and parents, the center offers numerous reports, articles, and books for student researchers, including "Sexting and Youth: Achieving a Rational Approach," "Why Age and Identity Verification Will Not Work," and *Cyber-Safe Kids, Cyber-Savvy Teens.*

Centers for Disease Control and Prevention (CDC)
National Center for Injury Prevention and Control
4770 Buford Hwy. NE, MS F-63
Atlanta, GA 30341-3717

(800) 232-4636
e-mail: cdcinfo@cdc.gov
website: www.cdc.gov

The CDC is the federal agency responsible for monitoring and responding to public health threats in the United States. It lists physical bullying and social rejection as individual risk factors for youth violence, including school shootings and suicides. It conducts research on the causes, consequences, and prevention of cyberbullying and offers numerous reports and guides on the subject on its website.

Gay, Lesbian, and Straight Education Network (GLSEN)
90 Broad Street, 2nd Floor
New York, NY 10004
(212) 727-0135 • fax: (212) 727-0254
e-mail: glsen@glsen.org
website: www.glsen.org

Founded in 1990, GLSEN fosters healthy, safe school environments where every student is respected regardless of sexual orientation or identification. It is the oversight organization of more than four thousand school-based Gay-Straight Alliances (GSAs) and the sponsor of two antidiscrimination school events, the National Day of Silence and No Name-Calling Week. Its antibullying initiatives include the educational website ThinkB4YouSpeak.com and the monthly e-newsletter *Respect Report*. The GLSEN website offers research reports such as *From Teasing to Torment: School Climate in America: A National Report on School Bullying* and *Shared Differences: The Experiences of Lesbian, Gay, Bisexual, and Transgender Students of Color*, as well as an antibullying toolkit titled New Safe Space Kit.

Make a Difference for Kids
People's Bank of Mt. Washington
PO Box 95
Mt. Washington, KY 40047
e-mail: donna@makeadifferenceforkids.org
website: www.makeadifferenceforkids.org

This organization promotes awareness and prevention of cyberbullying and suicide through education. It was created in memory of Rachael

Neblett and Kristin Settles, two Kentucky teens who committed suicide as a result of being cyberbullied. The organization encourages kids contemplating suicide due to cyberbullying to call the National Suicide Prevention Lifeline at (800) 273-TALK (-8255).

Mental Health America
2000 N. Beauregard Street, 6th Floor
Alexandria, VA 22311
(703) 684-7722; toll-free: (800) 969-6642
e-mail: infoctr@mentalhealthamerica.net
website: www.nmha.org

Mental Health America (known from 1909 to 2006 as the National Mental Health Association) is a nonprofit education and advocacy network. The organization works to raise awareness of and to end discrimination against those with mental illnesses through legislation and litigation, public-service announcements, and health insurance reform. Opposing bullying is one aspect of its efforts to improve youth mental health; the organization publishes the fact sheet "Bullying: What to Do About It" and related material on recognizing signs of distress in children, helping children cope with stress, and preventing child and adolescent suicide.

National Center for Bullying Prevention
PACER Center
8161 Normandale Blvd.
Bloomington, MN 55437
(888) 248-0822 • fax: (952) 838-0199
website: www.pacer.org/bullying

Funded by the US Department of Education's Office of Special Education Programs, the center is an advocate for children with disabilities and all children subjected to bullying, from elementary through high school. Bullying and cyberbullying prevention resources (available in English, Spanish, Hmong, and Somali) include audio-video clips, reading lists, creative-writing exercises, group activities, and numerous downloadable handouts such as "Bullying Fast Facts." The center sponsors school and community workshops and events such as National Bullying Awareness Week each October.

National Crime Prevention Council (NCPC)
2345 Crystal Drive, Suite 500
Arlington, VA 22202
(202) 466-6272 • fax: (202) 296-1356
website: www.ncpc.org

The NCPC, a partnership of the US Department of Justice and private sponsors such as the Wireless Foundation and the Ad Council, was founded in 1979 to get citizens, especially youth, involved in crime prevention. It is best known for its televised public-service announcements (PSAs) and school-based programs featuring McGruff the Crime Dog. Its other novel approaches to addressing social problems include the Community Responses to Drug Abuse program and Youth Outreach for Victim Assistance program. The council's cyberbullying campaign includes a public-service ad contest (winning PSAs are viewable on its website), free antibullying banners that users can copy and paste into e-mails or social networking pages, the Be Safe and Sound in School program, and educational training manuals for youth and adults to manage bullying and intimidation. Downloadable resources include a range of podcasts and research papers, including the Harris Interactive poll Teens and Cyberbullying.

Olweus Bullying Prevention Program
Institute on Family and Neighborhood Life
Clemson University
158 Poole Agricultural Center
Clemson, SC 29634-0132
(864) 710-4562 • fax: (406)-862-8971
e-mail: nobully@clemson.edu
website: www.clemson.edu/olweus

The program, developed by noted Norwegian bullying researcher Dan Olweus in the 1980s, is a school-based intervention program designed to prevent or reduce bullying in elementary, middle, and junior high schools. It is endorsed as a model antibullying program by the federal government's Substance Abuse and Mental Health Services Administration and the Office of Juvenile Justice and Delinquency Prevention. How the program works, statistical outcomes, and studies of the effectiveness of this and other antibullying programs are available at its website.

Wired Safety

1 Bridge Street
Irvington-on-Hudson, NY 10533
(201) 463-8663 • fax: (201) 670-7002
e-mail: parry@aftab.com
websites: www.wiredsafety.org; www.stopcyberbullying.org

Under executive director Parry Aftab, Wired Safety is an Internet safety and help group that offers articles, activities, and advice designed for seven- to seventeen-year-olds on a range of issues, including cyberbullying, cyberstalking, and other forms of harassment. Resources include a Cyber911 Help Line, a cyberstalking poll, cyberbullying Q&As, and a speakers bureau. Information available on its websites covers Facebook privacy protection, how to handle sexting, building safe websites, and many other topics. Wired Safety also sponsors the annual WiredKids Summit on Capitol Hill; in a role reversal, tech-savvy teens get the chance there to present cybersafety research, raise cyberbullying issues, and tell industry and government leaders what they need to know about cybersafety.

For Further Reading

Books

Kowalski, Robin M., Patricia W. Agatston, and Susan P. Limber. *Cyberbullying: Bullying in the Digital Age.* 2nd ed. Malden, MA: Wiley-Blackwell, 2012. Several psychologists explore the issue of cyberbullying and offer the latest research for parents and educators.

Li, Qing, Donna Cross, and Peter K. Smith. *Cyberbullying in the Global Playground: Research from International Perspectives.* Malden, MA: Wiley-Blackwell, 2012. This book explores the phenomenon of cyberbullying from an international perspective and offers research on intervention and policy strategies.

Patchin, Justin W., and Sameer Hinduja. *School Climate 2.0: Preventing Cyberbullying and Sexting One Classroom at a Time.* Thousand Oaks, CA: Corwin, 2012. The authors provide an overview of cyberbullying and offer practical strategies for educators and community members for addressing the problem and creating environments that counteract bullying.

———. *Words Wound: Delete Cyberbullying and Make Kindness Go Viral.* Minneapolis: Free Spirit, 2013. Written by cyberbullying experts, this book offers real-life stories of cyberbullying, strategies for victims, and advice for students who want to combat cyberbullying in their schools.

Trolley, Barbara C., and Constance Hanel. *Cyber Kids, Cyber Bullying, Cyber Balance.* Thousand Oaks, CA: Corwin, 2009. This guide provides a resource for educators who want to prevent cyberbullying, identify the warning signs of bullying, and better their school climate in order to improve student learning.

Periodicals and Internet Sources

Bernstein, Marvin. "Cyberbullying Won't Be Stopped with Laws and Punishments. We Need to Get Involved," *Globe and Mail* (Toronto), May 7, 2013.

Chicago Tribune. "Bullying Is Cruel, but a Crime?," October 19, 2013.

Cummings, Larissa. "Cyber Bullying Is Every School's Responsibility," *Daily Telegraph* (London), June 18, 2010.

DiManno, Rosie. "Cyber-Bullying Is Too Mild a Term for Criminal Harassment," *Toronto Star*, October 19, 2012.

Hakes, Francey. "School Bullying's Chilling New Front," CNN, September 5, 2013. www.cnn.com.

Jernigan, Floyd. "Awareness by Adults Can Help Stop Cyber Bullying," *Nevada (MO) Daily Mail,* October 19, 2013.

Kendzior, Sarah. "Why Cyber-Bullying Endures," Al Jazeera, October 18, 2012. http://america.aljazeera.com.

Laitano, Luisa. "The School System's Role in Cyberbullying," Honors Ethical Issues and Life Choices, paper 23, 2013. http://diginole .lib.fsu.edu.

Patchin, Justin W. "Not Guilty? Implications for the Teens Charged with Bullying Rebecca Sedwick," Cyberbullying Research Center, November 22, 2013. http://cyberbullying.us.

Siebold, Steve. "Parents Should Be Charged Along with Kids in Bullying Cases," *Huffington Post*, October 21, 2013. www.huffington post.com.

Siner, Emily. "Why Spying on Our Kids to Solve Cyberbullying Might Not Work," National Public Radio, September 17, 2013. www.npr.org.

Sticca, Fabio, and Sonja Perren. "Is Cyberbullying Worse than Traditional Bullying?," *Journal of Youth and Adolescence*, May 2013.

USA Today. "Cyberbullying Calls for New Weapons: Our View," October 24, 2013.

Yu, Valerie. "Cyberbullying Epidemic Needs Solutions," *Daily Trojan* (University of Southern California), February 28, 2013. http:// dailytrojan.com.

Websites

Cyberbullying Research Center (http://cyberbullying.us). This website is a resource for students, parents, educators, and community members who are interested in obtaining the latest research about cyberbullying and ways to address the issue.

Delete Cyberbullying (www.deletecyberbullying.org). This website is part of a project that strives to educate students and parents about cyberbullying; the organization offers research information, outreach programs, and tips for bullying prevention.

National Conference of State Legislatures' Cyberbullying Page (www.ncsl.org/research/education/cyberbullying.aspx). This website offers resources about cyberbullying as well as a list of cyberbullying legislation that has been enacted across the country.

National Crime Prevention Council's Cyberbullying Page (www.ncpc.org/topics/cyberbullying). This website offers resources for youth and adults on how to manage bullying situations and prevent bullying from occurring in their communities.

STOMP Out Bullying (www.stompoutbullying.org). This website is part of a prevention campaign that focuses on reducing cyberbullying and digital abuse among youth.

StopBullying.gov (www.stopbullying.gov/cyberbullying/). Managed by the US Department of Health and Human Services, this website provides information about how to identify bullying behavior, who is at risk, and how to respond when bullying occurs.

A Thin Line (www.athinline.org). This is the website for MTV's A Thin Line campaign, which aims to empower youth to stop the spread of digital harassment and cyberbullying.

WeStopHate.org (http://westophate.org). This is the website of a nonprofit organization dedicated to raising the self-esteem of teens and putting a stop to bullying.

Index

Oslo, Norway, cyberbullying study, 32

Picture Credits

© Angela Hampton Picture Library/Alamy, 114
© Ben Molyneux People/Alamy, 72
© bikeriderlondon/Shutterstock.com, 25
© Blend Images/Alamy, 101
© BSIP SA/Alamy, 10
© David Grossman/Alamy, 95
© David Pereiras/Shutterstock.com, 77
© David S. Holloway/Getty Images, 82
© Howard Simmons/NY Daily News via Getty Images, 44
© Jane Williams/Alamy, 14
© Janine Wiedel Photolibrary/Alamy, 31
© Michael S. Gordon/The Republican/Landov, 47
© Monkey Business Images/Shutterstock.com, 86
© NetPics/Alamy, 110
© Phanie/Alamy, 57
© Rawdon Wyatt/Alamy, 68
© Sean Spencer/Alamy, 19
© SpeedKingz/Shutterstock.com, 62